DECADENCE OF FREEDOM
JACQUES RIVIÈRE'S PERCEPTION OF RUSSIAN MENTALITY

JEAN-PIERRE CAP

WITH A PREFACE BY
WILLIAM EDWARD BROWN

EAST EUROPEAN MONOGRAPHS, BOULDER
DISTRIBUTED BY COLUMBIA UNIVERSITY PRESS
NEW YORK

1984

EAST EUROPEAN MONOGRAPHS, NO.CXLIX

TO MY WIFE

CONTENTS

List of Illustrations

FOREWORD

For many centuries geographic, cultural, and historical factors prevented Slavic peoples and Russians in particular from playing a role commensurate with their numbers in the mainstream of European civilization. Great distances, religious differences, and the Tartar occupation presented enormous obstacles to the interactions which should have normally taken place between Eastern and Western Europeans.

Until the eighteenth century, the Russian Empire largely remained a mysterious land, and Western Europeans had not yet bothered to assess its growing potential. During the Enlightement, some of the French *Philosophes,* exasperated with the social and political systems of their country, practically romanticised distant and unknown Russia. Catherine II was imagined as a benevolent despot. Diderot and Voltaire praised her as the Semiramis of the North and drew attention to her empire.

From the time of her participation in the partition of Poland, the role of Russia increased rapidly. Catherine the Great's expansionist policies against the Turkish Empire, the powerful intervention of Russian armies in numerous campaigns against Napoleon and the débacle of the *Grande Armée* made Western Europeans and especially the French realize that Russia had suddenly emerged as a great power to be reckoned with. This happened before any diplomat or strategist had declared this to be the case. The French Revolutionist Delaunay d'Angers seems to have been the first in 1794 to have sounded the alarm. In his *Plan de pacification générale en Europe* he replaced the traditional reference to the Turkish peril by the Russian menace. Austria and England also realized the danger of Russia's expansion at the expense of the Ottoman Empire. Thus the French Revolution contributed to Russia's participation in European affairs. From 1815 to 1914, Western Europeans, and the French in particular, increasingly focused their attention on Russia, especially after the signing of the Franco-Russian Alliance. Russian art and literature were then deliberately included in the process of fostering an understanding between the two recently allied peoples. Significantly, the Vicomte de Vogüé who then published *Le Roman*

Russe (1886), was a diplomat who favored the new alliance. In the quarter century preceding World War I, Russian literature and finally Russian music and painting made a dramatic appearance and impact in France and Western Europe. Diaghilev's *Ballets Russes*, the vogue of Tolstoy, and the discovery of Dostoevsky by the French élite also contributed enormously to the unveiling of Russian culture to the world.

Jacques Rivière, one of the most genial critics of the time, bacame an enthusiastic admirer of Russian culture. Writing in the influential *Nouvelle Revue Française*, he contributed perhaps more than any one of his contemporaries to the accreditation and dissemination of Russian culture not merely as the creation of a great and powerful people but as a new, bold and dynamic presence at the forefront of European civilization. This fact alone, overlooked until now, deserves attention. Even more significantly, the impact of Russian music helped Rivière find his way and discover the most important trends in the maze of the pre-World War I avant-garde. However, his attitude towards Russian art, literature, and epsecially Dostoevsky did not remain static. It was influenced by historical events. When Rivière became a prisoner of war he lived in daily contact with Russian prisoners of war for almost three years in Germany. This did not diminish the esteem he had for the Russian people and their art. Later, however, the establishment of communism disappointed him profoundly, and it can be regarded as the principal factor in his disaffection, not only because he regarded communism as incompatible with his way of life and his view of the world but because he felt that the new Russia would be even more powerful and therefore an even greater threat to his country and to liberal democracy. Once again geopolitical considerations superseded cultural reality in the shaping of the image of Russia by the Western mind. In this sense Rivière's evolution was typical and for this reason especially worthy of study.

My debts are many and some are intangible. My deepest personal debt is to my friend W. Edward Brown whose diligent and critical reading of my entire manuscript as well as his encouragement were invaluable to me. I also wish to thank Dr. George G. Sause and the Lafayette College Committee on Advanced Study and Research for their help as well as Professors B. Hlynsky, A. Kipa and E.A. Pope, who answered a number of my questions. I am also indebted to Edward Petersons, Jeannine Cap, Ingrid and Peter Wood; as well as to Mary E. French and Lorraine Miller who so patiently and carefully typed the entire manuscript.

All translations, unless orherwise indicated, are by the author.

J. - P. C. Easton, Pennsylvania February 1984

BIOGRAPHICAL NOTE

1886	Jacques Rivière is born in Bordeaux on July 15.
1903	Begins his studies at Lycée Lakanal, Paris, and his friendship with Henri Alain-Fournier.
1905	Returns to Bordeaux where he prepares his *Licence ès Lettres*. Beginning of his correspondence with Alain-Fournier.
1907	Receives the *Licence* at Bordeaux during his military service. Begins to correspond with Paul Claudel.
1909	Marries Alain-Fournier's sister, Isabelle Fournier, on August 24.
1909-1911	Meets André Gide and begins to contribute to the *Nouvelle Revue Française*. Teaches at the Ecole Saint-Joseph des Tuileries and the Collège Stanislas. Receives the *Diplôme d'études supérieures* at the Sorbonne with a thesis on Fénelon.
1911-1914	Secretary of the *N.R.F.* from December 1909 until the war. Publishes numerous critical notes and essays.
1914	At the outbreak of the war is called up as a sergeant and sent to the front. Taken prisoner at the battle of Eton on August 24.
1914-1917	Prisoner of war at Köningsbrück in Saxony except for a month spent at the reprisals camp of Hüselberg in Hanover after his attempted escape in 1915.
1917	Interned in Switzerland in June 1917 where he recovers and gives a series of public lectures on literature.
1918	Repatriated in July. Publishes *L'Allemand*.
1919-1925	Editor of the *Nouvelle Revue Française*. Plays a key role in French letters through the dynamic and imaginative leadership he gives the *N.R.F.* Publishes his first novel *Aimée* in 1922.
1925	Dies on February 14.

PREFACE

However hard they may be to document scientifically, we all unhesitatingly accept the existence of national characteristics—the quick wit and pugnaciousness of the Irish, the orderliness and conformism of the German, American brashness and naïveté, and the like. Such qualities are certainly not innate—there are no specific genes for religious mysticism, parsimony, or a fantastic imagination, for example; they are the product of the innumerable components of a national culture which set it apart from all other national cultures—geography, climate, religion, form of government, prevailing economic relations, etc. The farther apart these determining factors of a culture may be from one another, the greater will be the differences of the national characteristics. We readily impute to the French as national characteristics: logicality, an analytical bent, and an impatience with vagueness and formlessness. These qualities stand in almost diametrical opposition to some of those that seem to typify the Russian. There has always been, therefore, between these two nations the ambivalence that accompanies such divergence of character: a great difficulty of mutual understanding, and at the same time a certain reciprocal fascination, the attraction of opposites.

Jean Pierre Cap's study of Jacques Rivière, a typical French intellectual, in his quest for an understanding of the Russian character, reveals both the difficulty and the fascination of the quest, and his several avenues of approach: first through translated literature, then through music and art, and finally through direct contact with the people and learning their language. Rivière's experience illustrates also another aspect of the matter: drastic changes in some of the determining cultural factors, such as the economic and the political, can quite rapidly alter certain national characteristics; Rivière found the Russian under the Soviet government a different man from the one he had learned to know only a few years earlier in a German prison camp. National characteristics, though stable in the main, are not immutable.

How is a person of one culture to apprehend the qualities that belong to another? Intimate personal contact for a long time is of course the

14

best means. Failing that, however, a nation's cultural artifacts reveal much to an observant stranger. Literature, music, painting, sculpture, architecture, studied with an open mind, can be a surrogate for direct person to person contact. For peoples no longer existent, such as the ancient Greeks and Egyptians, this is indeed our only means of understanding. Even where direct contacts are possible and easy, no full understanding is ever possible without recourse to such intellectual means. The most complete understanding which is possible will be obtained, as in Rivière's case, by a combination of the two approaches.

Over the centuries of coexistence in the same world two peoples are bound to attempt to appropriate some of each other's cultural heritage. Translations and criticism wil be made of literary works, music and ballet will be performed in each other's country, paintings will be transported from one to the other. As a preliminary to studying the twentieth-century Frenchman's quest for "the Russian soul," it may not be amiss to have a brief look at some of the more significant earlier contacts between the two peoples in the realms of literature, music and art.

Cultural relations between France and what was to become Russia began, so far as we know, in the eleventh century, when Anna, daughter of Iaroslav the Wise, Great Prince of Kiev, married (c.1051) Henri I, King of France. It is significant that when the royal couple signed the marriage contract, the well-educated Princess signed her full name, while the King of France had to make do with an X. Kiev, heir to the age-old civilization of Byzantium, stood on a far higher cultural level than the half-barbarous Western World, and in any exchanges in the eleventh century between the two worlds, it would have been France that received and Kiev that gave.

The positions, however, were soon reversed when the Russian lands fell after the middle of the thirteenth century under the yoke of the barbarous Muslim Tartars, where they languished for some two hundred years. In this interval France became politically and culturally one of the leading powers of Europe, while the new Muscovite Tsardom which succeeded the principality of Kiev stagnated in a cultural backwater, cut off from both Byzantium and the West. By the time Tsar Alexei and his energetic son Peter resumed contacts with the West, Muscovy was decidedly on the receiving end. The famous "window on Europe" which Peter the Great had to open was not merely political but far more cultural. With Peter's daughter Elizabeth this window began to admit primarily French air, and an era began when the Russian upper classes became so Gallomanic that there was serious danger of their losing contact altogether with their own common people.

The reigns of Empress Elizabeth and her succesor Catherine II mark the high point of French cultural hegemony in Russia. There is significance in the fact that the man who is quite generally credited with being the founder of modern Russian literature, Antiokh Kantemir, published his famous Satires in France, in his own French translation, and it was only after his death that the original Russian text was published in his own country. Russian classical literature gives the appearance of being wholly derivative: dramatists such as Sumarokov model themselves on Racine and Molière; fabulists ape La Fontaine; epic writers find inspiration in Voltaire's *La Henriade*; and toward the end of the eighteenth century the "tearful comedy" of Nivelle de la Chaussée and Jean Jacques Rousseau's sentimental novel *Julie ou la nouvelle Héloïse* supplant earlier classical models. Actually, of course, even in this most imitative period, Russian literature retained remarkable originality.

The French dominance in Russian eighteenth-century culture was not unchallenged. From Kantemir on almost every satirist or comic poet ridiculed French affectations of dress, eating and drinking habits, drawing-room gallantry, and linguistic mannerisms. Fonvizin's *Brigadier* and Krylov's *Fashion Shop* are particularly vigorous and effective blasts against Gallomania. They were largely ignored, however, until political events changed the cultural climate.

Tolstoi, in the opening chapters of *War and Peace*, pictures the bewilderment of Moscow society when Russia's first war with Napoleon had suddenly made it unpatriotic to speak French. Ladies like his Anna Pavlovna Schérer complained, not without justification, that there were many things which simply could not be said in Russian. The language, adequate for the illiterate masses and for a literate class of ecclesiastics, was unequal to the demands of an élite educated in western ways.

For a period in the early nineteenth century French influence in Russia was eclipsed by German and English, but it never disappeared wholly, even in the years of active warfare between the two countries. It returned in full force when after the Revolution of 1789 hordes of French refugees sought safety in Russia and found employment typically as tutors in noble families. Young ladies and gentlemen in Moscow and St. Petersburg learned French from their earliest childhood, and usually employed it in social gatherings and in correspondence, in preference to Russian, which they often spoke and wrote very badly. A large proportion of the letters of, e.g., Pushkin and Lermontov, especially those addressed to ladies, is written in French; and it may be recalled that Tolstoi, in his first version of *War and Peace*, felt obliged to write about a third of the dialogue in French in order to convey the atmosphere of 1807-12.

During all this period, when upper-class Russia was so much a cultural satellite of France, the association was very one-sided. Voltaire could carry on, from a safe distance, an admiring and witty correspondence with Catherine II, and Diderot could actually make the arduous journey to St. Petersburg to meet in person the famous "Semiramis of the North." These contacts, however, seem to have remained on a quite superficial level: neither Voltaire nor Diderot give evidence of much real understanding of Russia and Russian culture—indeed, if the truth be told, neither does the German Catherine!

The advent of Alexander Pushkin (1799-1837) marks the beginning of Russia's genuinely national literature. Almost single-handedly Pushkin welded the disparate components of the Russian upper-class speech into a viable literary language. Although Pushkin's own prose style remained strikingly French, even specifically Voltairean, its lexical texture is Russian through and through, and after him there begins a cultural movement that slowly reverses the former position: France at last begins to learn that there *is* a culture in "barbarous Muscovy." Acceptance of this fact did not, however, immediately engender either sympathy or understanding. Joseph de Maistre, long time resident in St. Petersburg, was perversly sympathetic with Russian autocracy, but with little else. The Marquis de Custine (1790-1857) outraged Nikolai I and delighted Russian liberals by his caustic comments on despotism in Russia and the ignorance and barbarism of the Russian gentry, but he was woefully ignorant of Russian arts and letters and failed to appreciate the greatness and originality of Pushkin. Some other French littérateurs were more perspicacious, e.g., Xavier Marmier (1809-1854), who not only familiarzed a French audience with German romantics, particularly E.T.A. Hoffmann, but with Russian romantics as well (Pushkin, Lermontov, Viazemsky).

One of the important dates in Franco-Russian cultural relations is 1820-21, when French liberal leaders Benjamin Constant, Jouy, and M.-A. Julien de Paris arranged a series of lectures in the Paris Athénée by the young Russian poet Wilhelm Küchelbecker. In these lectures, given in French, Küchelbecker tried to interpret his people, their language, and their new romantic literature to his French auditors. They were very well received, but Russian authorities speedily recalled the too-bold lecturer and exiled him to the Caucacus.

Not very long after Küchelbecker's lectures Prosper Mérimée made his debut in French literature. His relations with the Slavic world began with a typical mystification: the publication in 1825 of *La Guzla*, a collection of alleged translations of "Illyrian," i.e., Yugoslavian, popular songs. This collection, which was actually original compositions of Mérimée's own modelled on Serbian ballads, was put into Russian verse by Alexander Pushkin, who was at first unaware of the hoax. Subsequent contacts between the two men led to Mérimée's excellent translation of Pushkin's story *The Queen of Spades* and his poem *The Gypsies*. Gogol's *Inspector General* and some of Turgeniev were also made accesible to French readers by Mérimée, and in later years he wrote a general critique of Gogol's work, which unfortunately he neither understood nor liked. Pushkin, with his clarity and balance, was far more to the Frenchman's taste.

The sensational death of Russia's greatest poet in a duel in 1837 led to a spate of articles in France and Germany by would-be interpreters of Pushkin and his importance as the creator of modern Russian literature. A leader of these interpreters was the former Jacobin Marc-Antoine Julien de Paris, editor (1819-31) of the *Revue encyclopédique,* whose journal, in close collaboration with Polevoi's *Moscow Telegraph*, carried a large number of reviews of works of Pushkin, Krylov, and even of such older figures as Karamzin, Derzhavin and Zhukovsky. Some of this material was contributed by the liberal Russian poet Prince Peter A. Viazemsky, anonymously, of course.

The novelist Ivan S. Turgeniev, as is well known, lived a large part of his life in Western Europe and died at Bougival near Paris. His long association with French men of letters did more than anything else in the nineteenth century to familiarize literary France with Russian achievements. A case in point is the translation (1845) of five of Gogol's stories by Louis Viardot. Turgeniev's curious symbiosis with the Viardot family is a familiar fact, and it was the Russian novelist who evidently did most of the translating, for Viardot knew Russian very imperfectly. Turgeniev doubtless also had a hand in the excellent article on Gogol which forms a foreword to the revised edition of Viardot's translation, and which can be said, along with Sainte-Beuve's 1845 article in the *Revue des Deux Mondes*, to have first given the French reader a true picture of that enigmatic but peculiarly Russian genius. Numerous unsigned French articles on Russian literature in *L'Illustration, Revue des Deux Mondes,* et al., written under the evident inspiration of the Russian liberal critic Belinsky, are also in all probability by Turgeniev. Turgeniev occupies a uniquely intermediate position, on the one hand as interpreter of his country's literature to a French audience, on the other as a pupil of French masters of the novel in his own works. Turgeniev's novels are distinguished among

Russian specimens of their kind by orderliness, concision, and clarity —qualities typically French and seldom to be encountered in Russian novels—those "huge baggy monsters," as Henry James characterized them. It is no accident that for the novelists who figure in Eugène-Melchior de Vogüé's *Le Roman russe* (1886), Turgeniev is, in the author's words, "entirely good." He had distinct reservations about Gogol, Dostoevsky, and Tolstoi, but Turgeniev strikes him as almost French. De Vogüé's attitude, it may be remarked, has been general among his countrymen. Jacques Rivière's delight in the dark qualities of Dostoevsky and the primitivism and savagery of Stravinsky's *Sacre du Printemps* is most exceptional.

Before de Vogüé's *Le Roman russe*, probably the profoundest and most understanding French evaluation of contemporary Russian literature is to be found in the 1847 article in *Revue des Deux Mondes* by Charles de St. Julien, a former lecturer on French literature in the St. Petersburg University. Not only does St. Julien do justice to Pushkin, whose genius was by now quite recognized in France, but also to Lermontov, who was hardly known at all, and to Gogol, whom Mérimée so misunderstood and underrated.

By the date of Gogol's death (1852) the "Pushkin era" of Russian literature was over and the era of the great novelists begun. It may be said that by this date literary France was quite well informed about the two greatest figures of Russian literature of the first half of the century, Pushkin and Gogol. Lermontov makes a poor third, but at least his *Demon*, *The Novice*, some of his best lyrics, and his novel *A Hero of Our Time* had been translated and his importance assessed. And yet France knew a great deal more about Russian cultural life at this time than did other European countries; England, for example, was abysmally ignorant on the subject. It is typical that as late as the 1870s an English publisher could issue Turgeniev's *A King Lear of the Steppes* in a translation not from the Russian, but from a French version!

The second half of the nineteenth century in Russia is dominated by prose, as the first half had been by verse, and the realistic novel holds first place in it. This novel found its first major interpreter in the work cited above by Eugène-Melchior, Vicomte de Vogüé. De Vogüé had served as secretary of the French Embassy in St. Petersburg and had married a Russian lady. Although his knowledge of the language was not perfect, and he knew some of the lesser figures and works only at second hand, he was quite well equiped to present his countrymen with a general overview of Russian literature—for this his work is, in effect, adequate   in spite of the limitations of its title. De Vogüé was personally acquainted with Turgeniev and Dostoevsky, and although like most

Frenchmen of his time he had little sympathy or appreciation of the latter, he endeavored to be fair to him and did somewhat reluctantly acknowledge his genius. His book was of course written over twenty years before Tolstoi's death and so deals only with the earlier novels and stories, through the date of *Anna Karenina*. Needless to say, de Vogüé views Tosltoi's religious aberrations with regret and feels that the master has abandoned his true sphere of activity for a fantastic and chimerical mission. The principal deficiency of de Vogüé's pioneering work is the exclusive concentration on the giants of the Russian novel. Goncharov, who is certainly a worthy companion of Turgeniev, Dostoevsky, and Tolstoi, is accorded only a sentence, with mention only of his novel *Oblomov;* Pisemsky, Saltykov-Shchedrin, Melnikov-Pechersky, and the dramatist Ostrovsky have about a line apiece, and the highly original and brilliant Leskov is not even mentioned. Nevertheless de Vogüé must be given great credit for having provided his countrymen not only with a generally fair and objective view of the major figures of Russian literature in the first eighty years of the nineteenth century, but also with a sketch of the complicated social and intellectual history of the time, the Decembrist movement, the Slavophile-Westernizer controversy, the Nihilist and Populist movements and so forth. Although de Vogüé is predictably unsympathetic with such typically un-French qualities in Russia's literature as melancholy, irrationalism, awkwardness, and pro-lixity (he complains of the "interminable length" of *The Brothers Kara-mazov!*), he is generally a fair and sometimes very perceptive critic.

The last twenty years of the nineteenth century saw a rapid decline in the dominant fashion of realism, which heralded the advent of the new wave of symbolism and a new age of poetry. Russian symbolism, e.g., Merezhkovsky, Gippius, Viacheslav Ivanov, Alexander Blok, and Andrei Bely, although it owes an immense debt to the French symbo-lists, runs a quite different course: it contains an admixture of religious mysticism that is quite foreign to, e.g., Rimbaud or Mallarmé. There were direct contacts between the movements, however, e.g., Valerii Briusov with René Ghil, but in general the Silver Age of Russian poetry was introduced to France only by the October Revolution and the re-sulting exodus of so many of its major figures to Western Europe, parti-cularly Paris. One of the last important prosaists of the realistic period, Ivan Bunin, lived the last of his life in France; the Merezhkovskys (Dmi-tri and his brilliant wife Zinaida Gippius) emigrated permanently, An-drei Bely temporarily; Balmont died in Paris; and Ivanov ended his life in Rome, a Catholic. The movement had flickered out in Russia itself even before the First World War, to be succeeded by other modernist movements which belong to a period beyond the scope of this essay.

20

Literature, especially prose literature, is the readiest of the arts to pass from one cultural realm to another. It might perhaps be expected that music, which is often called "a universal language," could perform this feat even more easily, but this is not the case. A book can be read, in private, by any literate person, and once a translation has been made of the foreign work, it is accesible to another people, not entirely undistorted, to be sure but it needs no interpreter, but the more ambitious it is —symphony, concerto, opera or the like—the greater the difficulties in its transmission, even within its own cultural realm. A simple song with piano accompaniment, a piano sonata, a violin solo—such things can readily enough pass from one sphere to another, wherever a musical amateur can be found to perform them. But works that require an orchestra, an operatic troupe, or a virtuoso instrumentalist will get no hearing without such performers to create them for a public. Few indeed are the specialists who can "hear" music by reading a score. It follows, therefore, that generally speaking it is only the great urban centers that before the advent of the phonograph and the radio were ever in position to hear anything but the simplest kind of music; and even there music's acceptance is always limited to the few hundred who have the interest and the financial resources to attend concerts.

It can be no surprise, therefore, that the French reading public was familiar with Russia's great writers many decades before Russian music was ever even heard of, much less appreciated. It is interesting in this connection to note a contrasting case. France traditionally has always had more sympathy with Poland than with Poland's conqueror and oppressor. Perhaps this sympathy goes back to the sixteenth century when it was possible for a Valois prince to be elected King of Poland; but in any case it becomes active after the partitions of the eighteenth century. The valiant but hopeless Polish revolts of 1830 and 1863 and their brutal suppression by Russian arms particularly elicited French sympathy. Polish refugees gravitated naturally to France after 1831—the great poets Adam Mickiewicz and Juliusz Slovacki, and the great composer and pianist Frédéric Chopin. Chopin composed almost exclusively for the piano and was himself a brilliant performer of his own works. His music won popularity in France at the very time when Mikhail Glinka was also a visitor in Paris; but Glinka was a composer primarily of operas and orchestral music—and besides, he was a Russian. Although Berlioz put him "in the first rank of outstanding composers" and praised his orchestration as having "the most modern and vital tone of our time," his music remained unknown to the French general public. Even more is this the case with Dargomyzhsky, whose visit in 1844 to Paris made no stir at all in French musical circles.

The first Russian composer to have an effect even remotely comparable to that of Chopin in France was the great pianist, Listz's rival and successor, Anton Rubinstein. Rubinstein made concert tours annually from 1853 to 1862, when his duties as director of the St. Petersburg Conservatory brought these to a temporary end. In these concerts he naturally played a great deal of his own music, and as an orchestra conductor he occasionally performed works by Glinka or other Russians. In 1885 and 1886 Rubinstein had a vast European success with his "historical concerts," in which he outlined the history of post-medieval music in a series of seven concerts, the last of which was devoted to the modern Russians—himself and his brother Nikolai, Glinka, Tchaikovsky, and even a number of the *kuchka* (the "Mighty Five," as they called themselves), Balakirev, Borodin, César Cui, Mussorgsky, and Rimsky-Korsakov, with whom Rubinstein was personally not much in sympathy. French, at least Parisian, audiences at last had an opportunity thus of hearing a sampling of Russian music, but this was of course by no means the best or the most characteristic of it, since most of the composers represented, even Anton Rubinstein himself, were at their best in orchestral works and operas.

Rubinstein's acceptance in France and the rest of Europe was primarily as a piano virtuoso; the best of his own music remained unknown. Peter Ilyich Tchaikovsky, on the other hand, won immense popularity in France, Germany, and England as a composer of symphonic music, ballets, string quartets, et al., quite without the adventitious glamor associated with a great performer. After the *Fourth Symphony* (1878) and his *Symphonic Suites* (the 1880s), he made a triumphant foreign tour, which included Paris, and was lionized (1888). Camille Saint-Saëns praised the " piquant charms and dazzling fireworks" of his tone poem *Francesca da Rimini*. Tchaikovsky's music should indeed have appealed to French tastes, for apart from his idol Mozart it was such French composers as Bizet and Delibes who chiefly inspired him. He paid some tribute to the Russian nationalist vogue, e.g., *Marche Slave, 1812 Overture*, etc., and took most of his opera subjects from Russian literature and history, e.g., *Eugene Onegin, Pique-Dame, Mazeppa,* etc., but his style was international and he remained isolated in the musical conflict that divided Russia in his time.

It should be noted that the ideological dichotomy which separated Russian nineteenth-century intellectuals into two warring groups of Slavophiles and Westernizers also had its counterpart in music. Thus Dargomyzhsky was strongly opposed to the prevalent French opera types of his day, the "grand" (e.g., Meyerbeer) and the "lyric" (e.g., Massenet, Delibes, et al.), and composed his *Rusalka* and *Stone Guest* in a highly original fashion, with emphasis on the natural cadences of words, to the neglect of melody. Rubinstein, Alexander Serov, and Tchaikovsky, on the other hand, followed the French models, using native Russian themes but treating them conventionally. The "Mighty Five," for their part, followed Dargomyzhsky and were strongly nationalistic: their inspiration, if foreign at all, came rather from Wagner, especially in their rejection of the conventional divisions of an opera into a series of set pieces—arias, cavatinas, duets, et al. Such music, even had a French public had an opportunity of hearing it in the 1870s and 1880s, before Debussy's musical revolution, would have won no acceptance at all. Debussy, it may be noted, became acquainted with Mussorgsky's *Boris Godunov* (a piano score) at the *Exposition universelle* of 1889 and was greatly impressed. This may be regarded as the first real breakthrough in Franco-Russian musical relations. The score he procured of the great Mussorgsky opera was of course Rimsky-Korsakov's rearranged and reorchestrated version, not the stark and powerful original, but in its revised form it was doubtless a good deal more readily assimilable.

Sergei Diaghilev's second Parisian venture (1907) was, as we shall see from Jacques Rivière's enthusiastic reviews, the real beginning of French assimilation of Russian music. It is interesting to note that by this time the music that was presented, and which met with tumultuous French applause, was almost exclusively that of the "Five": *Boris Godunov* in 1907, Borodin's *Prince Igor* in 1909, and Rimsky-Korsakov's *Pskovitianka (Ivan le Terrible)* in 1908. The only exceptions were an excerpt from Serov's *Judith* and the overture to Glinka's *Ruslan and Liudmila*. One might have expected, perhaps, such relatively "western" works as Rubinstein's *Demon* or Tchaikovsky's *Eugene Onegin*; but by 1907 France had accepted Debussy and Wagner, and Tchaikovsky's music, at first so popular (the symphonic music at least), had fallen into disfavor. The time was ripe for the aggresively nationalistic music of the Balakirev group, which was soon to be augmented by the brilliant young composers Igor Stravinsky and Sergei Prokofiev.

By their material nature, the plastic arts are least readily exportable from one culture to another. Individual collectors may accumulate fairly representative showings of painting or sculpture, but until or unless such collections become accessible in museums, or at least in public exhibitions, they remain a private treasure. Russian painting, for various reasons, has never until this century attracted any attention outside of the country. There are no western collections of Russian painting worth mentioning, and even the greatest artists and the closest to western artistic currents are unknown to this day in the western world. Russian collectors from Catherine the Great to Pavel Tretiakov amassed impressive numbers of French masterpieces: even today one of the finest collections of French impressionists is to be found in the Hermitage in Leningrad; but no French amateur bought up the works of Repin or Levitan or Vrubel, and the first revelation of this unknown world to a French public was Diaghilev's 1906 exhibition at the *Salon d'Automne* in Paris. This was a representative aggregation, ranging from some rather inferior icons to contemporary canvasses by Diaghilev's friends Larionov and Goncharova, and including quite a few of the best examples of Russian portraiture, which Diaghilev had borrowed from all over Russia for his immense exhibit in St. Petersburg the year before. The only artistic period or trend unrepresented was that very significant and fertile one dominated in the 1860s-1880s by the so-called *Peredvizhniki* or "Itinerants." These were rebels against academic art who abhorred élitism and were determined to bring art to the people. Their name comes from their unconventional practice of putting on exhibitions of their work in provincial towns all over Russia. Their art was aggresively realist and often contained a thinly veiled message of political or social protest. For them content and "message" were paramount, and they regarded painterly technique and style as unworthy of attention. Such tendencies were anathema to the "World of Art" group which Diaghilev represented.

The Russian realist painters were not, however, altogether unknown to the Parisian public. Although many of the most notable of them studied abroad, especially in Paris, they did not often achieve the distinction of a Parisian exhibition of their work. A notable exception is Vasili Vereshchagin, who in 1879 and again in 1881 exhibited a large sampling of his work—chiefly scenes from India and from the Russian wars in Central Asia and the Balkans—at a private gallery in Paris with resounding success, largely through the good offices of Ivan Turgeniev. Vereshchagin was a realist of the Itinerant school and an outspoken pacifist. His paintings coarse, badly composed and garish in coloring, and photographically detailed, exploit the horrors of war; they were most effective as propaganda, however bad as art, and it is likely that their open condemnation of the Balkan War of 1877-78, which alarmed the French, had a great deal to do with the success of Vereshchagin's exhibitions. The artist, it may be remarked incidentally, accompanied Admiral Rozhdestvensky's ill-fated fleet and lost his life when the Japanese annihilated it in 1905 at Tsushima Strait.

The exhibition of 1906 was Diaghilev's only attempt to bring Russian painting as such to the French public; but his ballets and operas in 1907 and following years incidentally familiarized the audiences with a great many of the most important artists of that anti-realist, neo-romantic, or symbolist group who were gathered around the publication *Mir Iskusstva* or "World of Art" (1898-1904). Thus Alexander Benois designed costumes and sets for *Le Pavillon d'Armide* and *Giselle*, and for Stravinsky's *Petrushka;* the antiquarian and ethnographic artist Nikolai Roerich for Borodin's *Prince Igor* and Stravinsky's *Sacre du Printemps;* Konstantin Korovin for *Le Festin;* Léon Bakst for *Cléopâtre, Le Carnaval* and *Scheherazade;* and Alexander Golovin for *The Firebird.* These were all major artists, and it was a great innovation of the "World of Art" group for such people to be engaged for what had hitherto been considered the rather secondary and menial task of scene and costume designing. Diaghilev continued the practice even after the war and revolution cut him and his group off from their homeland: Picasso and Matisse are among the western artists who contributed sets, curtains, etc. to the *Ballets russes.* A most notable feature of the earlier Diaghilev ballets was the extraordinary integration of sets and costumes, music, and dancing into a superb artistic whole.

Such, then, was the state of French acquaintance with Russian artistic achievements at the beginning of the twentieth century whenJacques Rivière began his quest. Literature was best served in translations from good to abominable, and in critical articles of considerable range and depth; but a literature is never truly represented by only its highest peaks. Very often the truest picture of a national culture will be found in its secondary or even third-rate writers—and of these in the case of Russia France was, and remained, profoundly ignorant. Poetry, moreover, which is always difficult to transmute into another language, was scarcely represented at all. Jacques Rivière made, so far as we know, no attempt to read any of the Russian writers but the great prosaists. Music was represented by a brilliant but narrow group—the ultra-nationalistic "Five" and the rather eclectic Tchaikovsky. Most of the rest of Russian nineteenth-century music, and all of the rich heritage of the ecclesiastical music of earlier centuries, remained unknown. Of the vast treasury of Russian painting, France, like the rest of Europe, knew only what little Diaghilev's ballets and operas imported in the way of scene design and such a second-rate and atypical body of work as Vereshchagin's. On the basis of such an inadequate and spotty sampling, how well could even such an acute and sympathetic observer as Rivière divine the national character of the Russian people? The answer will be found in Jean-Pierre Cap's admirably lucid account. Rivière's was a gallant attempt to accomplish the impossible. A certain defect in his manner of approach toward criticism, viz., a prevailing subjectivity and over-refined impressionism in lieu of logical analysis, vitiates some of his earlier essays; and the results which he obtains are inevitably based on too little material to be entirely valid. Nevertheless he deserves great credit for having made the attempt at all, and France remains in his debt for an interpretation which, if erroneous in some respects, as Jean-Pierre Cap points out, is correct in many, and is in any case the most comprehensive made in his generation.

William Edward Brown
Professor Emeritus of Languages
Lafayette College

In order to understand foreigners, a certain shyness is necessary. One must not be sure, at first, that one is right...

Even more is needed: some prior belief in the diversity of human nature, in the possibility of multiple fulfillment for the human being.

Jacques Rivière

I. THE RUSSIANS IDEALIZED 1905-1914

Jacques Rivière's Perception of Russian Mentality through the Arts (1905-1914)

An evident correlation exists between the power a country can exert on the international scene and the interest its culture elicits at a given time. This has been especially true of Russia as its image changed in the eyes of Western Europeans in general and the French in particular. Although Napoleon I had invaded most of European Russia, and Tsar Alexander I's Cossacks camped on the Champs-Elysées, French interest in Russia did not become serious and intense until the 1880s. Several writers did speculate on the future role of Russia with apprehension. Many remembered then Herder's prediction of a great destiny for the Slavs, whom he had foreseen as the future dominant power in Europe; others such as Heine and Herzen saw Europe's salvation through Russia. Taking stock of its rising power, Chateaubriand envisaged an alliance between France and Russia. Before this came to pass, however, Russia was to have a rather bad press in France for the greater part of the 19th century. After each of their unsuccessful attempts to free Poland from Russia in 1830, 1848, and 1863, waves of Polish patriots including such great figures as Chopin and Mickiewicz fled to France to escape Russian reprisals. As one might expect, many of them spread an extremely negative propaganda against the oppressors of their country.

Curiously, whereas Western and French Romantics sought exotic thrills on the periphery of northern and southern Europe and in distant and newly-discovered lands, for the most part they neglected those populated by Slavic peoples.[1] This was largely due no doubt to ignorance of Slavic peoples and their civilizations, but also to the old and deep prejudice felt by Western Europeans toward them. In the case of the French, the Russians' acceptance or toleration of despotism appeared as most unworthy of a civilized people. This was the basis in 1843 of the severe indictment of Russian civilization by the Marquis de Custine, whose opinions held sway for almost half a century. Of course the Crimean War (1854-1856) was to poison Franco-Russian relations even more for approximately a decade.

With a few exceptions, the French began to show a genuine interest in Russia when its political weight and potential began not only to be perceived but directly needed. There is a correlation between the catastrophic outcome of the Franco-Prussian War and the surge of interest in Russia which is noticeable in France after 1871. If the alliance between France and Russia then seen as a necessity was to become reality, the people, or at least the elite, had to become acquainted with the principal attainments of Russian culture.

Between 1893 and 1914 Russian literature, music, and dance did rise enormously in the esteem of the French to whom Russian culture had heretofore been unfamiliar. The Russian people, however, continued to be imagined as an uncultured mass. In this context, it is to Jacques Rivière's credit to have been one of the few acute and sympathetic students of both Russian thought and Russian art before World War I.[2]

Jacques Rivière (1886-1925), whom Paul Claudel referred to as "the ideal reader" and Henri Peyre as one of the three most important critics of the first half of 20th century, was guided by a sure instinct to the most beautiful and the most significant not only in literature but in music and painting as well. It is not surprising therefore that he should have sensed both the greatness and the innovations in Russian music and ballet on which he wrote with fervor and intelligence.[3] What is less known is that World War I made him focus his attention on the most important political trends and events as well: the rise of socialism, the Russian Revolution, and the necessity to put an end to the Franco-German duel. Whereas Rivière's writings on the Germans have inspired extensive commentary,[4] insufficient attention has been paid to his thoughts on the Russian people. Even thought some of his observations on their character and on their Revolution may be unoriginal, or even erroneous, a substantial number of them remain valid. All have at least a documentary value.

Rivière revealed himself most while writing on others. Their influence on him is fully apparent in literary encounters. Accordingly, the important essays he wrote on such figures as Claudel, Gide, Baudelaire, Rimbaud, and Proust have been carefully studied by his biographers and critics. Perhaps because his comments on Dostoevsky are brief and dispersed, the influence of the Russian novelist on Rivière has been all but overlooked or treated peripherally. Henri Peyre very aptly wrote that "surprisingly enough, the full history of Dostoevsky's impact on several countries of Western Europe and of America appears to have tempted very few scholars in the last three or four decades."[5] Yet Rivière was interested in Dostoevsky for almost his entire adult life and very keenly so from 1909 to 1917. For several years prior to World War I, while he elaborated his concept of the novel, the Russian writer's influence was perhaps dominant, as it was at times during his captivity in Germany (1914-1917). During these periods Dostoevsky was not only an esthetic inspiration to him but a spiritual one as well. He also contributed perhaps more than anyone else to the French writer's awakening to the great political issues facing Europe. When at last he wrote an extremely perceptive essay on Dostoevsky, in 1922, Rivière also recognized that "maybe he would always consider the time he spent in his intimacy as the best in his life."[6] However, by then his attitude toward Dostoevsky and the Russians in general had changed. The three years he spent with Russians in a prisoner-of-war camp had enabled him to observe them at will and to learn their language. In spite of the defects he was able to notice, he did not withdraw his sympathy from the Russian people; but he no longer saw them predestined to play so great a role in the destiny of Europe, nor did he wish that to be possible.

The turning point in his attitude towards the Russians came in the spring of 1917 as a consequence of the Russian Revolution. For a time he suppressed his fervent preference for Western liberal democracy and attempted to consider the Russians' experiment in socialism with understanding. Later, however, increased knowledge about the Revolution, and especially the separate peace of Brest-Litovsk signed by the Soviets which to him amounted to a betrayal of the Allies, caused Rivière to become severely critical of both socialism and of the Russians themselves. This reaction should be understood in this context. Rivière was too close to the situation and too emotionally involved to be objective.[7]

*

Rivière's observations, criticism, and reflections on the Russians can best be studied in the context of the following three important periods of his life:

(1) from 1905 to 1914 when with increasing admiration he studied Russia in general through Moussorgsky's and Stravinsky's music, and through literature, especially Dostoevsky's works;

(2) from 1914 to 1917 when he studied the Russian personality by observing Russian prisoners of war, learning the Russian language, and reading Tolstoy, Gogol, and Dostoevsky;

(3) from the early months of 1917 to 1925, the period of his disillusionment with the Russians because they had opted for a social and political regime which he loathed. With regret he thought that it corresponded to their personality which he found lacking in dignity and

will to strive for the establishment of a political system favoring individualism. Even his admiration of Dostoevsky then began to suffer from his disaffection.

Nevertheless, Rivière's deep, sympathetic, and sustained interest in the Russian people and many aspects of their culture resulted in profound interpretations and insights, some of which remain valid in our time. His attitude towards the Russians was quite unusual among French and Western observers and critics. To many Russians' satisfaction, he can be regarded to have been for a time a quasi-antithesis of the Marquis de Custine.

*

It is interesting to note how Jacques Rivière was attracted by the rather distant Slavs who continued to be ignored and often scorned by Western Europeans. While still a student, and on his own initiative, Jacques Rivière first came into contact with Russian culture through its literature and music. His correspondence with his friend and future brother-in-law Henri Alain-Fournier (1886-1914)[8] is our best published source of information on his early activities and thoughts. In it we learn that by the summer of 1905 he had begun to read Tolstoy (R-F, I, 110). His interest in Russian music had also been awakened, for the same year he wrote that he would have liked to have heard Balakirev's *Russia* (R-F, I, 120). Until the outbreak of World War I Rivière's interest in Russia and his knowledge of its culture continued to grow.

By the first decade of the 20th century, outstanding Russian achievements in all areas had made Custine's severe criticism of a half-century earlier appear undeserved.[9] In fact, Russia had been asserting herself in French cultural circles since the 1880s. The first book in French on the Russian novel, *Le Roman russe*, 1886, by the Marquis Eugène de Vogüé (1848-1910), had been quite widely read both in France and abroad. Political reasons also explain the increased interest of the French in Russia. By signing a treaty of alliance with Russia in 1894, France had succeeded in breaking out of the diplomatic isolation in which Bismarck had maintained her. The Russo-Japanese War and the subsequent Revolution of 1905 made a strong impact on Western Europeans. Frenchmen especially were shaken by the defeat of their ally and by the progress of socialism in Russia where they were investing very heavily at that time. These developments were not lost on Rivière, nor were Fournier's occasional epistolary comments on the revolutionary ferment among the Russian people. While studying in Bordeaux in 1905-1907, he had for a time frequented a Socialist circle which he did not find stimulating. Political concerns were then of secondary importance to him. Until World War I Russian music and literature, especially Dostoevsky, elicited his deep interest in all aspects of Russian culture accessible to him.

At twenty, under the influence of Paul Claudel who was then serving in China as consul, the very sensitive Rivière had thought of seeking new surroundings in Japan instead of attempting to pursue a career as professor of Greek or philosophy. For him Asia was then powerfully attractive. It was, as he wrote, the *alma mater* (R-F, I, 202). Soon his vision of Russia and that of Asia were telescoped. One should bear in mind, however, that Rivière—a true heir to Greek and Roman civilization—was not fascinated by Asia as the mainspring of civilization itself. Instead, it apeared to him at first as a vast, mysterious, and primitive land where man originated and also where he might still be communing with nature in ways unaltered by civilization. As with so many of his contemporaries who looked back with nostalgia to the dawn of man, he too was very strongly attracted by the purity he imagined existed in primitiveness. Was he not to write in 1908, "happiness is the first gaze on the marvelous earth" (R-F, II, 254)? When the words "brutal," "frightful," and "primitive" appear—and they do frequently—in his comments on Russia, they are not used in a derogatory sense but with a shiver of delight. This reaction is best explained not by an immature yearning for exoticism or for adventure, but by a self-defense reflex, which will be observed at work in other circumstances of his life. The fear of and excessively great impact on his individuality always caused him to turn away from a writer he idolized and to be attracted by one with different views. Thus one might say that to some extent Rivière turned to or was attracted by a putative Russian "primitivism" because he felt oppressed by Western and more precisely French sophistication. It could be said that he longed for a certain naturalness or even plainness. When thrown into the then rough conditions of military life, he wrote: "I now perceive the barbaric beauty of the service...What is beautiful is life with brutes... At last, I am reconstituting my primitive soul" (R-F, I, 290). Not surprisingly, he liked the later Gauguin. In 1910, referring to his favorite painting by him, Rivière wrote: "I am thinking of this large canvas, of this strange Paradise of meditation which Gauguin entitles: 'What are we? Where do we come from? Where are we going?'" There is a correspondence between the painter's art and Rivière's fascination for all that was both "avant-garde" and "primitive" (R-F, I, 389).

Another constant in Rivière's taste as a young man was his liking of all that is dark, mysterious, and unfathomable. For example, in *Anna Karenina*, which had not overwhelmed him, he did find "two or three admirably dark passages" (R-F, II, 69). What he saw as mysterious were aspects of Russian personality which soon made Rivière become thoroughly infatuated with Dostoevsky.

On August 5, 1907 he began reading Dostoevsky's *The House of the Dead*, which did not immediately conquer him. But after having finished it on August 29, he wrote one of his longer epistolary commentaries on a literary work:

> The Dostoevsky [*The House of the Dead*] is truly poignant. It is painful to read because of the repetitions, the confusion and the infinite quantity of detail. He does not skip anything. But at times, the Russian people appear mystical, mocking, servile, brutal, incoherent and gratuitous. There is a terrible story: "Akoulina's Husband," which is told by the convict. From one end to the other the hero acts in a kind of continuous drunkenness. And all that he does that is willful and premeditated is completely gratuitous, without reason, almost without intention.
>
> At times, the servility of these people is revolting (even Dostoevsky's who accepts a whole lot of horrible things almost without protesting). But he who feels it (the servility) to be so true, so natural, so in the blood, appreciates him more.
>
> There are admirable types. [...]
> There are scenes. [...]
> It is beautiful. Now I must read a novel by him. (R-F, II, 160)

From this passage, as well as many others, one can infer that what he read by a Russian writer, Rivière regarded as a document or at least a source of information on the Russian people rather than merely as a source of esthetic pleasure which was his usual approach to literary works. Of all the defects Rivière noticed here in the Russian character, servility probably disappointed him most. Soon he read novels by Dostoevsky and his admiration for his works grew. In fact the great Russian novelist's influence on Rivière was probably dominant for a time in 1912-1913.

Before the war, Rivière read at least all of Dostoevsky's major works, as well as those by several other Russian writers--always, it seems, with the hope of better understanding the Russians. Having read Gorki's *The Stormy Petrel*, he commented that the political passages are boring, although this does have in Russia a tragic dimension which is difficult to imagine in France. But there are one or two astonishing stories: "Le Réveillon" among them. It's so Russian! (R-F, II, 172)

It must be remembered that Rivière had never visited Russia, and he had probably never met a Russian! But already he had a vision of the country, which was exalting to him, especially in its "primitive" and tragic aspects. He also seemed to feel that Russia was destined to play a great historical role. Everything seemed to corroborate the notion of Russia he had then. For example, on seeing a Russian furniture exhibit, he found it to be "admirably barbaric, rich, and sumptuous" (R-F, II, 179).

However, Rivière's interest in Russian culture subsided for a time before more compelling concerns until the spring of 1908. It was then violently reawakened by *Boris Godunov* which inspired boundless admiration in him. He expressed this enthusiastically on 27 May 1908:

> Last night I went to hear *Boris Godunov*. I cannot tell you how beautiful it is.
>
> [...] Whereas *Pelléas* is French, *Boris* is Russian [...] It is not Russian in the way Rimsky's flashy and barbaric poems are, but Russian in a way which is unknown to us [...It] has the admirable barbarism of Gregorian...It is Russian in that it is of an unimaginable spontaneity, in that melodies spring up all of a sudden and whip you and envelop you like an unexpected blast of wind, and that in our time only a Russian barbarian could have [created] such musical primitivism. The melody is almost always so pure that it has the perfume of snow.
>
> In short, it is infinitely "closer to my heart" than all of Wagner. (R-F, II, 213)[10]

Mussorgsky's music was clearly an almost traumatic revelation for Rivière since he equated it with that produced by Debussy's *Pelléas et Mélisande* which until then had been his greatest esthetic experience. He loved Mussorgsky's music for its primitive purity and force, which he considered the basic elements of authentically Russian art and character. He marvelled at its anachronism which in his mind corresponded to Russian isolation and backwardness. His preference for Mussorgsky over Wagner is also symptomatic of his evolution away from symbolism, which he still admired. Several years hence he was to consider symbolism as dead. The impact of Russian music probably contributed to his esthetic evolution (as well as to that of other Frenchmen of this period). It doubtless also rekindled Rivière's interest in Dostoevsky about whom he noticed an article by André Gide.[11] But he was so overwhelmed by *Boris Godunov* that he resumed his dithyrambic praise of it.

> The choruses in *Boris Godunov* are extraordinary. I have never heard the likes of them. You have to see all these fellows and gals wearing superb and barbaric moujik costumes swarm in the court of the monastery or in a snow landscape, and sing, sing as choruses have never sung in France.
>
> I believe you would like the decor which is clumsy but sumptuous. The last scene, where Boris dies in the midst of terrible hallucinations, ends with the arrival of a procession of ambulatory catafalques. It is terrifying. (R-F, II, 213)

Again we note that far from being repelled, he was attracted by and admired that which is both "superb and barbaric," "clumsy and sumptuous," "powerful and primitive." No wonder that he saw Boris Godunov again at the earliest opportunity and a week later he wrote again to express his enthusiastic admiration:

> I believe that I will be saying Mussorgsky as I say Claudel or Debussy [who were then his greatest heroes....] The melody has a way of perpetually springing up like a fountain, the harmony has a way of always being so breathlessly refined and so simple and spontaneous that it dumbfounds you. I know I am exaggerating like the true southerner that I am. But in spite of all the cool resistance I try to oppose them, things like these thoroughly move me and compel me to shout. (R-F, II, 218)

After having acquired a thorough familiarity with Russian music, he did write extensively on it beginning in 1911 until the outbreak of World War I. Although his enthusiasm was motivated by different qualities in Russian music and by several composers and genres, it did not diminish in any way. Interestingly, to Rivière music appeared as a medium through which he felt the Russian people could best be understood. This is reflected in the numerous allusions he makes to their collective psychology. By contrast, as Marcel Raymond pointed out, when writing on German (or French) music, Rivière did not attempt to make ethnographic extrapolations. Probably no other people interested him more than the Russians.[12]

Rivière's deep involvement with Russian music eclipsed his interest in Russian literature until 1909, when he met André Gide. During the latter's first visit the subject was not only broached, but the two writers had a lengthy discussion on Dostoevsky. The following day Rivière wrote:

> Gide talked to me about Dostoevsky. He insisted that I not continue [reading] *The Eternal Husband*. He says: either it will distract [me in my] work or the contact will not be strong enough. I spoke to him of *The Idiot*. He told me that he never found anything useless in it, that all the lengthy passages seemed justified to him. He claims *The Possessed* is the most terrifying and the greatest [of Dostoevsky's works]. Formerly, Turgenev used to interest him. But he finds him too literary now, and quite small in Dostoevsky's shadow. (R-F, II, 267-268)

From his account of Gide's defense of Dostoevsky's technique we can infer that Rivière had objected to the Russian novelist's seemingly excessive use of details, which had already irked him when he was reading *The House of the Dead*. In 1922 he was to write that he had sobbed on hearing Gide read him a chapter from *The Brothers Kamazarov*. Thus we know that Rivière had been feeling his way in Dostoevsky's work and that in fact his first contact with it during the previous years had not been sufficiently effective. It was in 1910-1911 under both Gide's and Jacques Copeau's influence that Dostoevsky was to make his greatest impact on Rivière. Gide had a thorough knowledge of Dostoevsky's work. He admired the Russian writer perhaps above all other novelists and was writing his biography.[13] As for Copeau, who was becoming a very close friend of Rivière's, he was then immersed in the writing of an adaptation of *The Brothers Karamazov* for the stage.[14] Rivière soon shared both their enthusiastic admiration for Dostoevsky and to a considerable extent their interpretation of his works. When Copeau's adaptation was staged in 1911, Rivière wrote: "Every morning, while dressing, I imitate with Isabelle [his wife] the Kamazarov actors" (R-F, II, 382).

In his reviews of this financially unsuccessful production of Copeau's remarkable adaptation of *The Brothers Kamazarov*, Rivière included a brief analysis of Dostoevsky's technique. He was overwhelmed by the "extraordinary abundance" of the novel, though he no longer regarded this as a defect but as one of the "essential elements of its beauty." Like Gide, he then felt "no detail [was] useless," and he was convinced that Dostoevsky could evoke life only through "supreme complexity."[15] He was also deeply moved by the Russian novelist's spiritual depth. In his essay on faith, "De la Foi,"[16] (On Faith) published the following year, Rivière emphasized the metaphysical dimension of Dostoevsky's characters. It is in them and through them that he saw the unmistakable mark of God on man.

> Dostoevsky's characters attain from the start the ultimate depth. They are totally human but they also have all that man has from God. [...] They do all the evil they have to. But at last they reach the bottom; they find again in themselves the One which is nonetheless in all. [Even when he is in his worst disposition] there is in [a Dostoevsky character] something more than his sentiments: it is this weak image of God which does not quite disappear. ("De la Foi" 978)

It is in this divine imprint on man that Rivière saw the origin of the charity latent in Dostoevsky's characters.

> When two men meet [...] they recognize each other; they are brothers in Jesus Christ; charity suddenly surges in them. [...] For God is alive in them again; He is with them again and His infinite peace comes and goes between their souls, uniting them as it will unite all men after they will have been judged. ("De la Foi" 979-80)

Though not a practicing Christian at this date, Rivière was capable of a remarkably close identification with Dostoevsky's characters. There is no doubt that even then the latter had a powerful impact on Rivière's esthetic as well as on his spiritual development. In 1913 he was to write to Valéry Larbaud:

> As far as I am concerned, I can say almost without any exaggeration that my life is divided into two parts: before Dostoevsky, and after. Nothing stands next to him, and there is perhaps no greater saint than he.[17]

Rivière's enthusiasm for the Russian author was shared by Fournier who was then undergoing a religious crisis and was especially sensitive and responsive to Dostoevsky's mystical dimension as the following passage shows.

Since Claudel no book has brought me closer to Christianity than *The Idiot*. There is never a question of it and yet since I have read it, I am haunted more than ever by the "temptation" [to convert]. Maybe this book is the bridge between the Christian world and my own world for which I have long searched. Here and there, perceptible at times, is the deep country where freed souls recognize each other and [communicate]. (R-F, II, 296)

Several years later, when he experienced his own religious crisis, Rivière became even more sensitive to the mystical dimensions of Dostoevsky's works, and he also began to see them as a bridge to Christianity. But in 1909 he was not in such a frame of mind. In fact, he seemed annoyed at his brother-in-law's spiritual evolution, all the more so when he saw him turn to Charles Péguy. Though not a practicing Catholic at the time, Péguy was deeply religious and patriotic; but he was also a xenophobic writer who had a special grudge against the Russians, their autocratic regime, their intolerance, and their imperialism.[18] Significantly, in admonishing Fournier, Rivière invoked Dostoevsky against Péguy: "I wish you recognized that Péguy can be as monstrous as Claudel. For example his horror of Russians [...] is hard to swallow. I'd like very much for you to admit it [...]" (R-F, II, 380). The admiration he had for Dostoevsky doubtless made it intolerable for him that the Russian people be despised. However, his concern for Fournier's faithfulness to Russian culture was unwarranted, for when he came closer to conversion, he wrote that since Dostoevsky, Péguy was "probably and most evidently the man of God" (R-F, II 419).

From 1911 to 1914, Rivière's reactions to Dostoevsky cannot be as minutely documented. He did insert, however, an analysis of the Dostoevskian character in his essay "On Faith" and the following year, two of his most significant works of criticism dealt with Dostoevsky and Stravinsky.

The first of these essays, "Le Roman d'aventure,"[19] is not directly a study of existing fiction but an attempt to charter the "terra incognita" of fiction yet to be created and to guide novelists in their discovery of it. His purpose was not to guess what turn it was to take, but to elicit and help bring about the writing of a new kind of fiction. He had sensed that literature had cut its moorings from symbolism and was moving toward the high seas. He felt he could help it find its way by calling for a new kind of fiction. In fact, "Le Roman d'aventure" could be considered a literary manifesto. Throughout, Dostoevsky is on Rivière's mind and frequently the point of departure for his own theories even though he refers directly to the Russian novelists only a few times. His criticism of the symbolists "who knew only the pleasures of tired people," whom he contrasted with his generation, eager to enjoy "more violent and lively pleasures," reflected his personal taste for a dynamic life and art (*N.R.F. IX, 761-62*). Associating primitivism and force, Rivière again perceived Russians as having the strength and dynamism of a young people. To some extent, this explains why he was so attracted to them.

He was convinced, largely because of his admiration for Dostoevsky, that the new era would be that of the novel and drama as opposed to poetry, which had been the dominant genre of symbolism. From the outset he claimed that the new novel about to appear would "resemble none of those we know in French literature." To prove his point he went back to French classicism and more specifically to Descartes who had stated that a work of art had to be "perfectly finished in all its parts" (*N.R.F. IX, 914*). Instead of clarity and simplicity, he saw density and complexity as prerequisites of fulfillment.

> A given story, presented under a facile and limpid aspect, will need in order to reach its final plenitude, to encumber itself with a thousand strange and contradictory details, to cover itself with a thicker network of unjustifiable traits, to enter at last boldly in the regions of darkness. Is it not the case of almost all the episodes told by Dostoevsky? And who would dare say that they would be more finished by being simpler? (*N.R.F. IX, 923*)

Adopting what had first appeared to him as defects in Dostoevsky, Rivière insisted that in his mind "complex" did not mean confused or confusing. As he progressed in his description of the future novel, Dostoevsky's influence becomes even more evident: "First, it will be a long work, and a work in which there will even be some passages that drag" (*N.R.F. IX, 58*). He also saw the process of writing a novel not as one based on recollection, but on invention, not turned toward the past, but the future. "Reading such a novel would have to be an unforgettable event such as is the case with *Great Expectations, Wuthering Heights,* or *The Possessed*" (*N.R.F. X, 63*). In addition to a new adventure novel, Rivière also called for the advent in France of a new psychological novel such as Dostoevsky's to whom he gave an unfair advantage by contrasting him with Paul Bourget (*N.R.F. X, 69*).

For a time Rivière had not overcome his original reservation about Dostoevsky's art. He seems to have been justifying what had appeared to him as defects in the Russian novelist's works by repeating Gide's arguments which he had perhaps incompletely assimilated. Although Dostoevsky was the most frequently mentioned novelist in "Le Roman d'aventure," and was presented, if not as a model, as the most important ancestor and as the worthiest of being emulated by novelists of the future, Rivière did not write a major study on him. As we shall see, he was instead to state Dostoevsky's shortcomings in a postwar essay.

During the years immediately preceding the war Rivière did, however, write a number of articles on Russian music. These articles are significant as valuable musical criticism. They also help us understand how Rivière first attempted to penetrate the Russian soul through the medium of music. This approach expanded his psychological insight.

In his first study, on the Polovtsian scenes in *Prince Igor*, contrary to his usual approach, he did not merely analyze the music which he commented on with lyricism, or the musical technique which he considered unique, but expatiated upon that which *moved* him, "that which is most primitive in us." "These pages," he wrote, "awaken in our inner self the shapeless image of Asia." Through these scores he heard "a cheerfulness full of memories, a cadenced joy which is like the consolation of the most ancient regrets."[20] As after his initial exposure to *Boris Godunov*, three years earlier, or after his very first contact with Russian literature, he was again fascinated by a subjective notion of a Russian primitivism which delighted him because of its putative purity.

Rivière's article on *Boris Godunov* also possibly reveals more than an attempt at commenting on the musicological aspects of the great Russian opera. The young critic did not merely translate the feelings expressed by the music he heard, as he would when writing about composers of other nationalities, but through the music he attempted to imagine and understand the people who had inspired it:

> The curtain is raised, it is all of holy Russia that sings with
> its bells and its prayers. [...] Mussorgsky's melody is a story
> in humility, it ignores justice, it is a diaphanous litany, it is
> an enthusiasm full of naïveté, an inspiration laden with
> prayers...the advent of piety.[21]

He ended his article on a note revealing a quasi-mystical concept of brotherhood:

> Mussorgsky's music is the voice of Russia itself. Russia,
> our little mother in sorrow, our holy mother, praying, suffering, smiling! You speak to God for us. You are our ambassadress."[22]

To Rivière, Russia had acquired an added dimension. Not only was it barbaric and primitive but the country most endowed with redeeming Christian qualities. As with Heine, Hertzen, and Dostoevsky, Russia appeared to him to be destined to save the world, and the Russians had become the chosen people. Thus the rich folkloric elements of Mussorgsky's music so enchanted Rivière that he transcended the psychological level and reached the spiritual, even mystical. Since from a technical standpoint Borodin's and Mussorgsky's music did not present considerable innovation, its novelty to Rivière was in its exoticism.

By 1912 he had become aware of the important shift that was occurring in European art from symbolism to modernism. Henceforth, he was to write on contemporary Russian ballet and music. Still, paradoxically, it was this avant-garde art that most often evoked to him images of a primitive Russian people. During the same years, Gauguin[23] fascinated him as African sculpture interested other critics who were focusing on the avant-garde. Rivière was not drawn to the culture of primitive people, however, but to primitiveness distilled by art. In his article on Igor Stravinsky's *Petrushka,* the most avant-garde ballet produced at that time by Fokine's[24] dancers, Rivière affectionately referred to the Russians as "very dear children." This epithet is not patronizing here. On the contrary, he thought the West was "indebted to Russia for having restored the art of dance. Is it not (Russia) which seems to be destined to find again a naive use of so much wealth...?"[25] He was delighted in "a thousand delectable and coarse elements," "an admirable rusticity," its life and its naïveté. Curiously, the most positive image which the most modern Russian ballet inspired in him corresponded to the then prevalent stereotype about Russia. That which the vast majority of Europeans and Frenchmen considered as negative, however, he regarded as most admirable. More importantly, he was beginning to realize the relationship between what he referred to as "the vertiginous reality" of primitive times and the subconscious.[26] Accordingly, he wrote that in Fokine's ballets it was no longer a matter of Slavic "color, barbarism, or orientalism," as so many critics were repeating. He viewed Fokine's originality independently of exoticism. He understood his incontestable superiority and his genius. This attitude is confirmed in his long article on Stravinsky's *Rite of Spring*, where he protested against clichés such as "Orient! Thousand and One Nights! Persian miniatures!" which critics and public alike had pinned on the Russian dancers. Rivière correctly attributed this misunderstanding to ethnic differences, increased by cultural estrangement. "Between them and us," he explained, "there is the distance separating one race from another." He insisted, although not pejoratively, on the Russians' impermeability to French influence: "I was quite foolish to fear for [Fokine and his dancers], the contagiousness of Paris! Not a dent was made on this little troupe of men. They have lived in our midst, as if in the middle of a steppe."[27] It should be noted that he considered Fokine's dancers as a troupe, rather than a group of individuals, for he already had accepted the notion about the "fusion of souls" which he regarded as specifically applicable to the Russians. As we shall see, this idea, which Rivière was to develop, had apparently been suggested to him by Copeau who in 1910 had sojourned in Russia.[28] It was to have a profound and lasting influence on his understanding of the Russian mentality, even on his interpretation of the Russian Revolution, and ultimately it contributed to his disenchantment with Russia. At this time, with only a knowledge of Russian music and literature, he confidently explained his new-found theory as follows:

> With [Frenchmen or even Western Europeans in general] all is individual: a strong and characteristic work bears the mark of one spirit alone. It is not so with the Russians. It is impossible for them to communicate with us; when they are among themselves, they have an extraordinary ability to blend their souls and for several of them to feel and think the same thing. Their race is still too young [to have developed in each being] those thousand little differences, those delicate personal reservations, those light but impassable defenses which shelter the threshold of a cultured mind. Originality is not in them this fragile balance of heterogeneous sentiments which it is in us. There is something about it that is freer, rougher, less easy to damage. That is why it can for an instant become involved and lose itself in others. (*N. R. F. X, 311*)

This passage shows how keenly Rivière was interested in penetrating the mystery of the Russian personality. Like most Westerners at this time, he regarded the Russians as typical and representative of all Slavic peoples. He was to cling to his notion about the "fusion of the souls" which was to inspire his negative deductions. This is strange, for his conclusions were based on the observation of an art performed collectively and in which the fusion of individual roles is often imperative. Curiously he did not relate his thought to Jules Romains' theory of unanimism, which was familiar to him. Nevertheless his admiration for *The Rite of Spring* was enthusiastic. He considered it a breakthrough in art, and no critic praised it as lavishly as he did in the face of an outraged public.

Rivière found in Stravinsky's masterpiece the qualities which he had admired in other Russian works: "frank, intact, limpid and rough music" continually evolving in the realm of the extraordinary (*N.R.F. X, 706*). It was "a tissue of magic tricks and successes," and Stravinsky appeared to him "like an almighty enchanter" (*N.R.F. X, 711*). For a moment, he forgot he was a spectator in Paris

> The extraordinary story is transmitted to us; we take it in large easy pieces, like savages seated around the elder of the tribe who deals out openly the supernatural adventures of the gods. We thus listen to so many enormous inventions entering into our ears. Stravinsky is first and foremost the one who talks, the storyteller. In that, and in spite of differences in technique, he alone among Russian musicians resembles Mussorgsky. [...] Stravinsky's music is above all the voice of the *niania* [...][29] Even lost in the history of monstrous times, it is still our mother Russia which speaks to us and lavishes upon us the treasures of her immemorial innocence. (*N.R.F.* X, 714-15)

Stravinsky was revealing to Rivière not merely a Russia in a primitive state, but in a subconscious one or one anterior to consciousness. Just as in poetry, where Baudelaire and Rimbaud were helping him sense its existence and importance, Stravinsky was guiding him to a similar discovery in music. Of all living artists probably none contributed as much as Stravinsky to sharpen Rivière's perception for the momentous changes which were in the making in all the arts. However, in keeping with his already firmly anchored notion about the Russians' propensity to blend together, he went on to write:

> *The Rite of Spring* is a sociological ballet. It is the extraordinary vision of an age which heretofore we painfully had to reconstruct and which is now made perceptible to our imaginations. (*N.R.F. X, 728*)

The term "sociological ballet" is used because *The Rite of Spring* had enabled Rivière to imagine primitive man as a social being rather than as an individual, to conclude that gregariousness leading to the formation of society existed before individualism, and that to become an individual one must *leave* a group.

> We witness man's movements when he did not exist as an individual. Being still held together, [men] are caught in the

horrible indifference of society; they are dedicated to the god
which they together form and from which they have not yet
been able to untangle themselves. Nothing individual appears on their faces. At no instant of her dance does the
young woman betray the personal horror with which her
soul should be filled. She accomplishes a rite, she is absorbed by a social function and, without showing any sign of
comprehension or interpretation, she makes motions following the will and the impulses of a being vaster than herself, of a monster full of ignorance and appetites, full of
cruelty and darkness. There is Moloch brought back alive
from the depths of the oldest epochs. He quivers, he opens
his jaw before us. Oh god so low and without spirit! (*N. R. F.
X, 728-29*)

It is an extraordinary coincidence that Russian artists should have inspired Rivière at this time with the vision of a collective and totalitarian
society. It is also the most unfavorable light under which he had yet seen
Russians. He cherished individualism and regarded it as a more advanced stage in the evolution of man than collectivism. Accordingly, he was
deeply disappointed though not surprised to learn that the Russians resigned themselves to organized collectivism at the end of World War I.
In 1913, he felt such revulsion for collectivism that in concluding he
went a step further and considered Stravinsky's music--

a biological ballet. Not only is it man's most primitive dance:
it is a dance which precedes man. It is as if one were witness-
ing a drama under a microscope; it is the story of karyoki-
nesis, the obscure function of the kernel separating and re-
producing. (*N.R.F.* X, 729)

What Copeau had called "the fusion of souls" Rivière perceived not
only as a psychological phenomenon but as a social phenomenon as
well, one which inexorably brings about transformations in each individual analogous to biological metamorphoses. As a Catholic, he con-
cluded on a most pessimistic note: "For the first time I felt evolutionist
theory had a kind of despairing possibility...Ah! How far I was from humanity!" (*N.R.F. X, 730*). Thus Stravinsky's music and Nijinsky's[30]
choreography enabled Rivière to make such sociological and biological
extrapolations that he was led to consider man's condition from a strictly
materialistic point of view — man in his pre-human stage of evolution,
whereas until then he had been preoccupied by man's quintessence—his

spirit, his soul. Earlier in his study, Rivière clearly stated his debt to Stravinsky:

> For me it was the discovery of a new world...I was making in art a discovery which is analogous to that of geometry in the sciences, and the joy I felt was the same as the satisfaction given by a perfect demonstration. (*N.R.F. X, 716*)

As Marcel Raymond explains, Stravinsky helped Rivière understand avant-garde music.[31] This in turn prepared him more readily to perceive changes in the plastic arts, and in literature.

As usual, when writing about Russian music or literature, Rivière had gone from esthetic criticism to the psychological study of a people—a people for whom he had genuine sympathy. Once he had seen its primitivism as charming exoticism. Through Stravinsky's music he was able to understand much more significant implications.

The following year, in his third essay on Stravinsky,[32] he specifically recognized the principles of cubism and futurism in his music. Although he had been quite sarcastic about these movements in painting, he did not criticize the Russian composer for the musical revolution he was bringing about. In fact, he acclaimed him as "the creator *par excellence*" in contemporary music. However, by admitting that "at this time his inspiration [was] as naturally inhuman as that of Mussorgsky was naturally human," Rivière revealed a stand which he did not change (*N.R.F. X,158*). Although he did not always like what he discovered, he had a passion for being among the first to know and to understand.

In the first phase, that is to say until World War I, Rivière's interest in Russian literature and music grew until it reached its highest point in his enthusiastic admiration of Dostoevsky and in his long and important study of *The Rite of Spring*. In that study and even more so in his short appraisal of the 1913-1914 Russian musical season in Paris, one can sense some reservations which were probably due to his fundamentally antagonistic attitude to cubism and to the harbingers of surrealism. The fact remains that during the pre-war period two Russian artists had an important influence on the development of Rivière's esthetic ideas: Dostoevsky and Stravinsky.

NOTES

1   Among the major French authors of the nineteenth century, only René de Chateaubriand, Honoré de Balzac, Alphonse de Lamartine, Alexander Dumas (père), Prosper Mérimé and Charles Nodier did travel through some Slavic lands, mostly the Balkans. Balzac and Dumas, however, did visit Russia in 1858. Although Victor Hugo, Mérimé, Dumas, and Lamartine wrote on Russia, or borrowed Russian themes, few works of French nineteenth century literature were inspired by Slavic lands or people.

2   It should be noted, however, that Rivière did benefit from the work of such well informed writers as E. M. de Vogüé: *Le Roman russe* (1886); A. Leroy Beaulieu: *L'Empire des Tsars et des Russes* (1881-1888); Theodore de Wyzewa: *Ecrivains étrangers, 3e série: Le Roman contemporain à l'étranger* (1900); as well as from contemporaries such as André Suarès, André Gide, Jacques Copeau, Romain Rolland and Emile Faure.

3   A list of Rivière's writings on or partly on Slavic culture can be found in the bibliography at the end of this volume. Furthermore, the abundant documentation he accumulated clearly indicates that he intended to write a book on the subject.

4   Henri Peyre has written that *L'Allemand* was probably Rivière's most widely read work, and Lionel Richard has given a thorough historical account of Rivière's thought on the Germans and the German question in his "Jacques Rivière et l'Allemagne," *Ethnopsychologie,* XXXIX, March 1974, 51-80.

5   Henri Peyre: *French Literary Imagination and Dostoevsky and Other Essays,* University of Alabama Press, 1975, pp. 1-2. Peyre himself deals briefly with Rivière and Dostoevsky, 15-17.

6   Jacques Rivière, "De Dostoevsky et de l'insondable," *N.R.F. XVII* (February 1922), 175-178.

7   The war awakened in Rivière a keen interest in international politics. Before the war he never wrote on this subject, whereas afterwards, he published several major articles in the *Nouvelle Revue Française* and twenty-two on more specific topics in international politics in the *Luxemburger Zeitung* from 1922 onward.

8   Jacques Rivière and Henri Alain-Fournier, *Correspondance 1905-1914.* Nouvelle édition revue et augmentée, 2 vols. Paris: Gallimard, 1948. It will henceforth be referred to as R-F I or II.

9   Marquis Astolphe Louis Léonard de Custine, *La Russie en 1839,* Paris: Amyot, 1843.

10   Rivière wanted to become a music critic. Several years earlier he had envisaged writing a theory of music. He attended many performances of the same works both for his pleasure and to learn the scores by heart. For example, he attended *Pelléas et Mélisande* some twenty times! On the basis of Rivière's comments, my colleague, Professor William Edward Brown, concludes that Rivière probably saw Rimsky-Korsakov's version of the Russian opera: "In the original version the final scene is in the Kromy forest, with the entrance of the Pretender on a white horse, and all the people rushing off to follow him, while the Idiot sits by the dying camp fire and croons his melancholy song about the woes of poor Russia."

11   André Gide: "Dostoevsky d'après sa correspondance,"*Revue des Etudes franco-russes*, June 1908. This is included in Gide's *Dostoevsky* (Paris: Plon, 1923). The work was dedicated to Jacques Rivière.

12   Marcel Raymond, *Etudes sur Jacques Rivière* (Paris: Corti, 1972), 121.

13   Gide's book on Dostoevsky did not appear until 1923 (see note 11) and he never finished Dostoevsky's biography which he had accepted to write for Charles Péguy's *Cahiers de la Quinzaine*.

14   Jacques Copeau adapted *The Brothers Karamazov* in collaboration with Jean Croué. Their version was staged in 1911.

15   Jacques Rivière: *"Les Frères Karamazov au Théâtre des Arts," N.R.F., V* (May 1911), 757-760.

16   Rivière, "De la foi," *N.R.F.* VII (November - December 1912), 780-810 and 970-998.

17   Raymond, p.215.

18   Péguy was also incensed by Russian censorship which occasionally returned some of the issues of his *Cahiers de la Quinzaine*.

19   Jacques Rivière, "Le Roman d'aventure," *N.R.F. IX,* (May, June, 1913),748-65, 914-32; X (July, 1913), 56-77.

20   "Les Scènes Polovtsiennes du *Prince Igor* aux concerts Colonne," *N.R.F., V* (January 1911), 172.

21   "Moussorgsky," *N.R.F. V* (February 1911), 314.

22   *Ibid* p. 317.

23   Rivière wrote an essay on Paul Gauguin, *N.R.F.* III (June 1910), 738-743.

24   Michel Fokine (1880-1942), Russian dancer and choreographer who lived and worked in France from 1911 to 1914.

25   *"Petrouchka,* ballet d'Igor Stravinsky, Nicolas Roerich et Vaslav Nijinski (Théâtre des Champs-Elysées)" *N.R.F., X* (August 1913), 310.

26   After the War Rivière was among the first in France to understand the importance of Freud. His thoughts on the subject were gathered in *Quelques Progrès dans l'étude du coeur humain (Freud et Proust),* Paris: Librairie de France, 1926.

27   *"Le Sacre du Printemps,"* *N.R.F., X* (August 1914),310.

28   In his *Dostoevsky* (Paris: Plon, 1923, p.119), A. Gide also refers to this alleged particularity of the Russians, claiming that he learned about it in Hoffman's biography of Dostoevsky. Hoffmann, T. H. M. *Dostojewsky. Eine Biographische Studie.* (Berlin, 1899).

29   Nursemaid, an important figure in Russian life, folklore and literature.

30   Vaslav Nijinsky (1888-1950) was the greatest ballet dancer of his generation. He enjoyed a sensational success in Paris from 1909 to 1914, both as a dancer and choreographer. He choreographed *The Rite of Spring*. Rivière admired Nijinsky greatly.

31   Raymond, pp.169-181

32   "La Saison Russe: *Le Rossignol*," *N.R.F., XI* (July 1914), 150-162.

2. Rivière's Early Essays on Russian
Music, Ballet and literature

Since adolescence Rivière had shown a keen interest in all new developments in literature, music, and painting. He greeted enthusiastically the novelty which Russian music and dance represented for the Western European public. He was moved by the exotic beauty and spirituality of traditional Russian music which to a great extent coincided with the way he perceived the Russian spirit intuitively and through his reading of Dostoevsky. Diaghilev's Russian ballets had an even greater and more important impact on his taste and his comprehension of the evolution of modern art. Initially, they were pure enjoyment for him, but soon they helped him perceive the fundamental changes which were occurring in art and taste. His experience of Russian music contributed significantly to making him one of the most enthusiastic and perspicacious critics of innovative trends in European art in the first quarter of this century.

All of Rivière's essays on Russian music, ballet, and literature are presented chronologically, in the order in which they were published from 1911 to 1914.

The Polovtsian Scenes in *Prince Igor* by Borodin[1]
by Jacques Rivière

At once I can see Fokine with his troupe of archers. There is no music like these few pages of Borodin. They come and touch that which is more primitive within us, they awaken deep within us the shapeless image of Asia, the smothered memory of the great Mother.

Asia! Not the Asia taught to us by the Mediterranean and its ships, and which always smells of import trade. Land-bound Asia, I mean. It started moving through the steppes. It plods on foot by slow stages. It stops at night and dreams like those who travel without thinking of returning. The camp is set up. Fires. Tents. The night sparkles hard and blue. No sea as far as one can remember. Then, in the desertlike and distinct silence of the plateaus, arises a cheerfulness full of memory, a rhythmic joy like the consolation of the most ancient regrets. First I listen to those sad flutes which are joined, like the little steps which lead to the dance. I see those slow-moving groups which draw nearer to the gleam of campfires and under the night. And suddenly the immense, ravishing wave by which all are carried away, a melody like a violent yet fragile rain, a melody which sings in a rapid voice. It collapses like a flock of birds. It unwinds its bright lullaby and the women dancers as it unrolls are so well entrusted, so well hidden into its folds that they gently give rhythm to its absence when for an instant, like a memory which one takes the time to hold, it becomes quiet and vanishes. Meanwhile the men in turn leap forth, as if struck by a dream. Theirs is a deep and wild onslaught. The joy which moves them rises within them like a brutal dream. It shakes them, it makes them swirl in games which imitate something which they do not know and which has disappeared. That is the way in which they remember, that is the way in which they soothe their hearts. O music brusque, breathless, your rapture is stupor of melancholy. You are consolation through violence!

Lying motionless near the dancing areas, the leaders within their memories as low as vaults, see cities again.

NOTES

1   "Les Scènes Polovtsiennes du *Prince Igor* aux Concerts Colonne," *N.R.F.*, V (January 1911), 172-73.

Mussorgsky[1]
by Jacques Rivière

Panem nostrum quotidianum da nobis hodie.

As soon as in the prelude to *Boris Godunov* arises the poor, supplicating, and determined song, one can no longer be proud or pleased with oneself. This is the most naïve demand, the voice of hunger and thirst. I am drawn out of myself; all that is tight in me becomes unbound. Suddenly, I feel pity to be natural. It overflows from my heart without effort and shame. It frees me like tears. The curtain risen, it is all of holy Russia which sings with its bells and its prayers. It implores me; it is on its knees; it stretches its arms out; it calls me to witness; it addresses to me the chorus of its begging words. O! how well I understand its lament, how its pleading grips me!

Mussorgsky's melody is a tale of humility. Humility—not merely as a negative sentiment, the mere constraint of pride—but it is here, breathing, living, with a dear face which is both timid and bold. Under its inspiration melancholy speaks and prays. Right away it leaps; right away it opens its candid discourse. It is prompt like those unpremeditated words which need draws forth. It begins live and pure as a child who makes quick steps and clasps his hands. It escapes, it releases its thin and urgent song; already its soft and hasty breath blows. So sudden is its birth that it seems surprised. It is a sentence one has been unable to hold back. It has no thought. It did not wait to be understood. Thus its impatience is full of modesty. It is as ingenuous as wretchedness.

No fear, however, would be capable of stopping it. No shame, nor even abashment. The want which drives it on does not think of blushing. It does not claim anything either; it knows nothing of justice and does not demand in bitterness its due. What surge in the prayer! What confidence in the One toward whom the prayer rises! "Ask and you will be given...For whosoever asks receives." It is the voice of the child who is never turned down. It is living confidence. The melody is full of speed; hope whispers to it a thousand words at once, hope unties its long and agile phrases. It is manifold and active; it is clear precipitation, as in each and every leaf the wind speaking determines its notes and carries them away. It spends itself in living entreaties; it is entirely deliberate; it goes as fast as the language of the prayer; nothing interferes with the naïve generosity of its rapture. The imploring of the choruses is deliberate: they put a strange vivacity in their prayers. Even in the laments the bold rhythm does not cease. Xenia's lament is not a chant but live distress itself, in a virgin soul the sudden yearnings of despair, the sharp and timid grip of misfortune. There is quick dropping of the melody, a poignant letting go!

The melody does not consent to become shrouded anymore than to grow languid. Nothing blurs its limpidity. It is a line without shadows. It unfolds, completely surrounded by light, almost slender from being isolated by brightness. Sentiments, when they become very conscious, become full of implications. But here they are too new to tolerate any reticence. They are recited whole in a chant without restraints; they give themselves in one naïve phrase; they do not dream of enriching themselves through concealing. None of the detours, of the secrets and the allusions which make up western melodies. The musical phrase is without change or unevenness; it is illuminated by a uniform light; it offers all its parts without preference; it precipitates its syllables with equality. Shuisky tells of the massacre in which the Tsarevitch died. O what a diaphanous litany! Nothing but pure line, nothing but the terrible facts stated one after the other. The monotonous voice cries its affliction; full of anxiety and naked, it tells the story. One only hears its sorrowful speech which goes, distinct, without the support of any smothered tune, of any harmonic muting. It sings, solitary, of infinite love. The melody is as clear as love; like it, inside, it is completely full of light. It is all told, it no longer has any rests. It flows transparent and it is more delightful to the heart than pardon.

Harmony never swaddles or stifles the melody; for it is merely the radiance of its transparency; it is like the luminous haze which surrounds diaphanous bodies; it resounds as the wind throughout the day; it deepens only what is limpid.

This music is all action. In none of its parts is there slowness or twilight. Heavy and quenched sentiments are unknown to it. It is quite capable of suffering, but not of being sad. It has a clear conscience. How could pain prevent its joy? It has a kind of cheerfulness which is the very activity of its heart. It awakens, it smiles, it is like a child who speaks with all the words. O novelty of the soul! Nothing puts to sleep the dear cheerfulness of this music full of wonder. It is a naïve little flame, a vivaciousness which is tender even in distress. It is surprised, it is ravished. It turns to all things. It plays; it invents short and headlong stories. It is as bustling as joy, it's "got time but just barely."[2] Then it stops suddenly, preoccupied by the importance of a question which it is eager to pose. The ends of melodies are astonished and questioning.

This delicate turbulence seems to subsist even in solemnity. The latter is not marked by an orchestra slowed down by themes. It is not propped up by fanfares. It is but the widening of cheerfulness, but a phrase which opens and rises. It is enthusiasm full of naïveté, an inspiration charged with prayer, a triumph like an ample smile, the advent of piety. It is as happy as the gesture of the priest who, facing the crowd, opens his arms.

It is like the ease of soul filled with its own prayer. Never does it become pompous. It rules without grandiloquence. It remains joyous and modest as the words of an old man who professes Christ. It moves forth with the adornment of humility, it leans forward, it bows three times with its hands open forward.

Mussorgsky's music is Russia's voice itself. Oh Russia, little mother of us all in sorrow! Our holy mother praying, suffering, smiling! You speak to God for us. You are our ambassadress. You speak to him with all your words in *ia* and *shka*, in your long and humble phrases, in your language lively, low and supplicating. You are cheerful for us, you have hope for us. You alone know exactly what we are worth and you do not ask for more things than is our due. You are our best love and our best humility. We are committing our sins to you in order that you obtain our pardon. You are the woman sent to the terrible God, so that, having seen her, pitiful as she is, He will not be able to refuse us His mercy.

NOTES

1 "Moussorgski," *N.R.F.*, *V* (February 1911), 314-17.
2 The Children's Room, *Riding on a Stick*.

The Brothers Karamazov
by Jacques Copeau and Jean Croué
after Dostoevsky at the *Théâtre des Arts*[1]
by Jacques Rivière

Of the thousand reasons which seemed to make a dramatic transcription of *The Brothers Karamazov* impossible, here is, I think the most serious: the extraordinary abundance of the novel which is one of the essential elements of its beauty; it wouldn't be what it is, one of the most overpowering masterpieces of literature, if it were a hundred pages shorter. One finds in it a number of passages which are useless to the plot, strange dissertations, secondary episodes (*The Boys*), an immense philosophical discussion between Ivan and Aliosha, which some have felt could be detached from the main drama. No novel is made to tempt pruners more, as well as those who, while reading a book, first dream complacently of the cuts that could be made in it. Yet no detail is useless. Dostoevsky's works are not among those which lend themselves to be simplified without damage. An almost frightful life animates them, and each of these characters holds turned toward us his humble and violent face. We must understand that the least page we would remove from the book would dampen its ardor. This attempt has been made, and precisely on *The Karamazovs.* Who has not felt ill at ease and disappointed reading certain recent translations shamelessly abridged? The reason for the fading which the slightest suppression causes to the work is easy to discover: Dostoevsky succeeds in awakening life only by dint of complicating and loading his plot. He does not sketch it and enliven it with several neat and unadorned traits; it begins to throb only from the moment when it reaches its supreme complexity. And is it not time to understand the extent to which complication is an important literary value? Simplicity is generality. The more a work becomes complex, the more it becomes particular and thereby, the more it lives. One must not listen to the laziness of the few who dread "tangled" books. If the novel *The Brothers Karamazov* appears so formidably real, it is because it is written without any sacrifice. The greatest number of episodes, the very mass of events and moments, their indescribable intertwining gives the work a frightful existence and presence.

But theatre is the art of sacrificing. The novel can become drama only if it abandons all that was episodic about it. And this is where Messrs. Jacques Copeau and Jean Croué have given proof of profound ability and intelligence. They have been able to find the dramatic equivalent of Dostoevsky's complexity. They have neither tried to transport the complete work to the stage nor to analyze it to the point of having only the

55

digest of what was tragic. The plot of their drama is far from being simple. Critics have all experienced a great and very natural difficulty in telling it to their readers. Some declared that they were giving up summarizing the play. *The Boys* aside, the authors have indeed kept the triple story which the novel offered: the drama—half wedged in the past—which is played out between Ivan and Dimitri around Katerina Ivanovna; the rivalry between Dmitri and his father, to which the fierce desire they both have for Grushenka gives rise; finally the hesitation regarding the responsibility for the assasination of the old man. However, not even for an instant is the play unclear; one follows it from beginning to end without difficulty. The tragic line is of an admirable neatness. There is no division of interest; everything is caught up in the same movement. How can one explain that such complex events, such diverse relationships among characters so numerous, preserve, although deprived of the commentaries and details of the novel, a perfect clarity? It is because they are illuminated by the characters. Instead of the episodes of the drama coming to inform us about the souls of the actors, it is the actors who help us understand what happens. Indeed, as soon as each of them appears, he is alive, he is an individual, he is incomparable. We doubtless still have quite a few things to learn about him, and we would not be able to guess what he will do. But there he is, present—him, and not anyone else. And all occasions on which we are going to encounter him, as strange, as little prepared as his gesture might be, we will still understand him—for this one reason that this gesture will have been his. He will carry everywhere the light of his personality. Merely by appearing in it he will unravel all the intricacies of a given episode. We may be quite at a loss if we are asked why a given adventure appears so natural to us; and if we should have to justify it logically, it will appear ridiculous to us. Where is indeed the link between Dmitri's and Katerina's story and Dmitri's and Grushenka's loves if not in Dmitri himself? And why will we accept the fact that instead of Dmitri, it is Smerdiakov who killed the father, if not because we see Smerdiakov himself, with his air of ignobility at once avenged and broken which the great actor Dullin gives him, and we see him aproach Ivan, raising his eyes at last?

In a more abstract fashion, one could say: it is because the authors have been able to give each character his entire complexity, that the complexity of events is so easy to unravel. They have used one complication to clear up the next. They have combined so well the numerous and contrary traits of each figure that they have formed an individual who rose and who began living with a unique soul, letting us see, as if radiating them from himself, his hidden and delicate relations with all the others.

In a work that succeeds so nobly, what do the few shortcomings matter—which one overlooks anyhow? The fourth act may appear too much a mere tableau; as a character Katerina is somewhat abandoned in the fifth act...But these are details which do not count. The two authors have given proof of such knowledge of the theater in this adaptation that we must expect, not necessarily more from their collaboration, but from their individual efforts, personal works of the highest order.

NOTES

1 *"Les Frères Karamazov* au Théâtre des Arts," *N.R.F.,* *V* (May 1911), 757-60.

Petrushka, ballet by Igor Stravinsky,
Alexandre Fokine and Alexandre Benois[1]
by Jacques Rivière

It is because we love the Russian dancers that we do not attempt to dissimulate their shortcomings and that we have reproached them for their error in *Narcisse*. But what a joy to be able after the reprimand to return to praise and again to indulge in admiration! For these Russians are very dear children whom one hastens to scold, so that one may tell them: "And now it [i.e., the scolding] is over; I find you lovable again."

Nothing resembles *Narcisse* less then *Petrushka*. One must call *Petrushka* a masterpiece; one of the most unforeseen, the most spontaneous, the nimblest and friskiest I know. How much work, planning, useless research in *Narcisse*! It seems that the authors exhausted themselves in piecing together discordant scraps of invention. Instead, *Petrushka* turns its nose up at such studious efforts and dances on one foot. One evening he is born all done, straight, ready; he is whole, frank, he does not know anything; with one leap he is on the edge of the stage, bustles and prances about. He had to come make us feel how rare fantasy is becoming. This ballet is fertile like one of Shakespeare's comedies; it has the same dash, the same health; it has the same soundness in its fancy; there is no arbitrary detail and in this extravagant world, everything is at each instant what it was supposed to be; I am perpetually surprised, and not once baffled.

The music by Igor Stravinsky; this name which *Firebird* taught us, we shall not forget. This young musician knows and handles with ease our modern orchestra which is so plodding and overburdened. But he does not try to be original by dint of little juxtapositions, of minuscule boldness, of fragile and unstable harmonic equilibriums. Instead, his boldness expresses itself in simplifications (in *Petrushka* there is an interlude which consists only of enormous blows on the bass drum). Without flinching, he ventures a thousand different kinds of delectable coarseness; he suppresses, he applies only frank and summary touches. He uses a trumpet and his find consists in using only it. He knows how to understate powerfully, and his vigor is made of all that he knows how to do without.

This decision gives his music an admirable rusticity, a bold and malicious cheerfulness. Now it is brusque and burlesque such as the crouching dance of the mujiks;[2] now it is full of a playful and familiar nobility in which irony consists only in a little dressing up for Sunday; it is in the appearance of the beautiful maidens, hand on hip, with their kerchiefs, who swing in their broad dresses whose colors are as sweet as those of images.

As for the dances, they were imagined by Fokine and they attest to true genius. This is where the man who knows how to feel his body at the tip of his soul finds a motive for rejoicing; here is the way to use all and every one of my limbs, here is the agility which they contain and can develop. Now I understand better what moves me so powerfully about dance: nothing plastic about it, no attitude, but to be able to see a human being leaning, taut, ready for the leap: and suddenly he moves forth, he runs, he turns, he raises his arms, he stirs, obeying frantically the hidden rhythms of his overflowing life. He strikes the ground with his foot. It is enough for my joy.

Dance is the art in which one creates with one's self, with the closest and most natural materials one could ever have to use of. We will owe to Russia to have relearned it. Does not Russia seem to be finding again a naïve use for so many riches with which we no longer know what to do?

NOTES

1   "*Petrouchka*, ballet d'Igor Stravinsky, Alexandre Fokine et Alexandre Benois" *N.R.F., VI* (September 1911), 376-77.

2   Rivière is referring to the dance of the Cossacks.

Russian Ballet and Fokine[1]
by Jacques Rivière

Quite a few people still have not understood that what should be admired in Russian ballet is dance. And how can one hold it against them when one sees this truth, however evident, being misunderstood by Nijinski himself? All manner of praise has been given to the Russian troupe except the one it deserved, the one which Fokine was certainly keen on receiving. Without rime or reason people have spoken of color, barbarism, orientalism; they have praised Stravinsky's music (one could not rank it too high), they have declared that Bakst[2] is a great genius. But they have not brought themselves to admire that which was unique about these shows, which made them different, not in quality but in character, from all those which we have been able to see until now. The public has not consented to feel a new emotion, to put itself in an artless frame of mind. It is as if it had watched in a miraculous state of blindness the prodigious novelty which had been unfolding before its eyes. It is because in general nothing frightens it more than to venture into undergoing a feeling which it does not know yet and for which it has no words.

Because, not having sought out the essence of what it had to give, some already accuse Russian ballet of having disappointed them, it is important that we indicate here precisely the solid element of these works, that which in them is not subject to fashion, which is eternal. Their richness alone prevents one from seeing their originality. Let us imagine that they are poor, let us suppress all their ornaments: we shall then show how that which remains is moving and that it alone can legitimately move us.

*

Let us first strip them without fear of their decor and costumes. That is not to say that these props are not often admirable, and even very useful: the decor as a support to and as a reflector of movement; the costumes, in order to free the line of the body and to restore its continuity. But formerly I have seen rehearsals of *Firebird* done in street clothes, and this year of *Daphnis et Chloé*. No experience could have been more decisive. On the stage, a man in shirt sleeves, having removed his detachable collar and put it on a chair, dances: that is enough. Each time he throws his legs backward while raising his arms in this grotesque and sublime fashion—I am referring to Dorcon's[3] comic dance—each time he makes these few steps, cleverly entangled and out of time with the music, I feel my heart beat, I feel the disturbance and the lightness of heart caused by admiration. I know my pleasure! It is real since it can exist by itself.

*

Meanwhile, one of our most prominent painters[4] was saying, speaking of ballet whose décor he had painted: "Did you see my piece?"

But now we must make a bolder suppression. It no longer is merely a question of removing from the dancer certain ornaments which are quite external and which he at times spontaneously renounces; what is important is to distinguish between his rest and his movement, and among the various uses he makes of his body, to accept only the way in which he animates it and throws it forward.

The human body can indeed touch us by its attitude alone and merely by a certain posture while motionless. Painters know it and they apply themselves to capturing attitudes. They catch their models' attitude at the instant where it ceases to move. They paint it inwardly abandoned by its motion, as a boat which touches sand, noses up gently and stops; they show it at the moment when it finds once more its own profile, that it seemed to be pursuing, recaptures it and lengthily kisses it, leaning against it. This profile, this attained limit, this line on which all momentum comes to a stop, we cannot view without pleasure.

Yet let us have courage against ourselves. Doubtless it is natural that a dancer should move us at times like a beautiful face within a painting. But this pleasure is not the one required of us here. Let us avoid it; or let us simply enjoy it as a bonus. In a dance, attitude is nothing. The dancer must attain it in the end lest he flutter about endlessly; but it is like a period at the end of a sentence: what counts is the sentence. The attitude marks the moment when one can applaud; but what one should applaud is not it, but that which it has interrupted. Everything is over not when the dancer leaves the attitude, but as soon as he falls into it, not when he rises and leaves, but as soon as he begins to be immobile.

That is where the critical point is. The same being suggests to us at the same time two emotions which are very different. One of them is long since known to us; it is the one we have felt at the sight of all masterpieces of painting and sculpture; the other is absolutely new. Hence we quite naturally fall back into the former, which is the easier for us.

It is therefore necessary to insist on the distinction we have sketched. With his body the dancer simultaneously traces two different kinds of figures: one which is outlined against the décor, the other which is etched against the background of our memory. At whatever moment one may catch him, like his shadow, a silhouette, very definite, very well marked, very clear. But at whatever moment one may catch him, he is also constructing with his movements another figure which is less distinguishable, as yet unfinished, and which one can guess rather than see. The first is in one piece; it is in space; it would stay there if we had the time to inscribe it on the backdrop by sketching it with one stroke of the pencil. But the other, even when it shall be complete, we shall not be able to sketch it, for it will remain fixed in time; it will be made up of a thousand successive gestures sewn together the way minutes are: all the forward movements, all the side-steps, all the about-faces of the line embroidering it will be linked together only in the invisible and will only have a meaning while imitating that of our memories.

*

It is this secret figure and not the other that we must admire; our pleasure must originate in it. But it is time to explain how it is admirable, time to confess at last why pure dance, stripped of all its ornaments, of all that enhances its seductiveness, still appears so delectable and so poignant to us.

Ah! how can this be made understandable to someone who does not already feel it? But is it possible that a man not feel all that of which his body is capable and that at the word "movement" alone he not be perturbed by a physical passion?

The dancer does not yet move; his head is slightly inclined forward, he is listening within himself to all the potentialities which go off, burst, subside because it is not yet time. There he is, on the lookout. But at last the music, like a vase that one waited to fill to the brim, suddenly is level with his body; it goes on; and there he goes with it, effortlessly, as a withdrawing wave might carry us off our feet. O uncontainable smile! O sudden freedom! O debate in a new world! Why should he force himself? He comes and goes, he bends down; he strikes the air with his arms; he playfully follows with his feet all these tiny descending notes; he touches the melody with his hands; it goes through him, it goes up in spirals which finally escape through the tips of his fingers; he runs after it when it leaves him, he picks it up again as one would play with an animal. He passes from one point to another, not haphazardly as you or I would, but his movement carries him like a slow angel; there is one movement which seizes him in the middle of a leap, which it stretches. He no longer needs his strength, for all the aptitudes of his body cease to be captive, and like liberated spirits, they fly in him; and he feels as if wafted by the fluttering of their wings.

And there he leaves me; I am forbidden to follow him; he travels on a path which he destroys as he passes over it: he goes along a mysterious thread which becomes invisible behind him: with this spreading gesture, with these hands which he moves in the air, with this body which turns gently and a thousand times, he seems like a magician busy trying to erase his track; we will not catch him; we will not succeed in holding him, in putting his arms against his hips in order to look at him at leisure, from head to toe. He enchants us, he baffles us, he carries our attention away with his hands, he is always as if at a turning point, and we follow his smile like a bird. He gives in before us, he grows faint, he goes away in such a fake flight that it ceaselessly seems on the verge of being defeated; he seduces us with a hope so near that we do not notice its perpetual deception and we so expect to capture his movements at last that we simultaneously forget all the movements he makes. That is why the desire does not leave us to see his dance again, to follow anew this vanished path, to return to the principle of this capricious error whose episodes faintly strive to come together again deep in our memories.

Fokine does not invent attitudes but movements. For if you are mistaken, if Rodin is mistaken, he is not. He knows that dance is the art of movement, that the dancer does not have to worry about pleasing painters with his attitudes and that he must remain free without ceasing to turn.

In order to understand how great an artist Fokine is, one has to have seen him from the auditorium, and for many hours, at work shaping his oeuvre on the stage from the movements which his dancers made available to him. How can one not feel moved by the modesty and the competence of this man? We have no control over him because he has a way of imagining that which is absolutely unknown to us. Something of which we have no idea occurs just next to us in his mind.

While absent-minded and faithful, he is attentive to this music which we, too, can hear; he sees movements. He smiles, his face seems younger, and his thoughts come to him as quickly as bacchantes. Some thoughts, suddenly and very rapidly, heads lowered and holding each other by the hand, pass very closely, in the forefront of his imagination. Others cover their faces with an elbow put forward, as if to hide laughter, and come from the depths, swinging, with gentle, untrustworthy glidings. A whole line of them crosses the stage, making great leaps toward the right; and from behind, another line flees toward the left and seems to put back in place as it comes up to it, one by one, all the motions of the first. Finally, as if behind a veil which is being torn, brusquely unmasked by this dance which is subsiding in the foreground, breaking away from the obscure regions of thought where for an instant they had been moving shapelessly, furious, full of tumult and bristling with gestures, like towers throwing javelins while turning, three solitary female dancers roll toward him.

This man visualizes all that is within him. Because there are yet no words to specify the nature of it, shall we refuse to recognize his genius?

NOTES

1 "Des Ballets Russes et de Fokine," *N.R.F., VIII* (July 1912), 174-80.

2 Léon Bakst (1866-1924), a Russian painter who became well known as a painter of scenery for some of the Russian ballets produced by Diaghilev.

3 "The face of the flower-picking maiden who sings
    Becomes so blurred in the thick dusk
    That only her eyes and her seemingly purple mouth
    appear."

Paul Claudel, *Tête d'Or,* p.292.
(Translated by J.-P. C.)

4 The painter mentioned here by Rivière cannot be identified.

Le Sacre du Printemps [I], Ballet by Igor Stravinsky,
Nicolas Roerich and Vaslav Nijinski
(Théâtre des Champs Elysées)[1]
by Jacques Rivière

This eighth "Russian season" (I am referring here to the ballet seasons) had begun in a somewhat disquieting fashion. In the first shows there was something undefinable which could have led us to believe that we were on the verge of decadence. If on the new stage of the Champs Elysées *Prince Igor* seemed all revived, on the other hand, the *Spectre de la Rose*[2], like too-delicate a flower, seemed to be dying from having been sniffed too often. *Jeux*[3] (whose case will have to be reviewed next year) was not likely to restore our courage. And I confess that Fokine's absence and the fact that his name no longer appeared on posters all quite but took away hope as far as I was concerned. I gave in to most pessimistic thoughts: "They have found their way, I thought, they now know what to do; they have shaped the public and all they need to do is slip into its ranks and take up their little collection. Henceforth, there is good understanding between the stage and the auditorium. All is clear, I therefore no longer have anything to do here." I could have ruminated a long time over this nonsense.

But all of a sudden, one evening, there was this gratuitous thing, this refusal to profit from the past, this terrible blow to the habits which they had formed in us, this work which changes everything, which modifies the very source of all our esthetic judgments and which we must count at once among the greatest: *Le Sacre du Printemps*.

Oh, you fine impervious minds! You did not hear anything of what was being said around you. At the performance of *Boris* you were in the auditorium, dressed in tuxedos, and people shook hands with you and introduced you over and over. And there was whispering around you: "Oriental! *The Thousand and One Nights!* Persian miniatures!" And you would answer: "Yes! Yes!" with a convinced air. But in the meantime you had this in your heads; for two years you had been quietly carrying within yourselves this revolting work which was going to draw shouts of horror from your most conditioned admirers! I was quite foolish to fear that you could be infected by Paris! This little troupe of men has not been impaired. They have lived among us as in the middle of the steppe. The air they breathe is not the same. It is not the same thoughts that are born in their brains. Between them and us there is all the distance from one race to another. Nothing from us will ever reach them. During the performances of the *Sacre*, absolutely deaf to the roars and whistles of the spectators,[4] Nijinski could only think of beating time with his foot while shouting to his performers: "It's soft! It's soft!" We must be convinced that for him we did not exist. Certainly no more than Stravinsky, did he risk anything in the tumult of our compliments. This was but a strange noise to his ears.

Who is the author of the *Sacre du Printemps*? Who made it? Nijinski, Stravinsky, or Roerich? This preliminary question which we cannot avoid has meaning only for us Westerners. In the West, everything is individual; a strong and characteristic work always bears the mark of a single mind. It is not so among Russians. If it is impossible for them to communicate with us when they are among themselves, they have an extraordinary ability to blend their souls, to be feeling and thinking the same thing in unison.* Their race is still too young to have had the time to develop those thousand little differences, the delicate personal privacy, and the light but impenetrable defenses which shelter the threshold of a cultured mind. Originality is not in their case the fragile equilibrium of heterogeneous sentiments which it is in ours. Their originality has something freer, rougher, less easily damageable. That is why it can penetrate that of others and for an instant lose itself in it. Let us take notice of the fact that for six years we have known the Russian troupe, yet we have not succeeded in knowing who the soul of it is, who among all those whose names we have learned is the creator. Last year, I thought it was Fokine; I was wrong, I mean, that he was not alone. I see now that one must believe the poster when it lists three names for a single work. The *Sacre du Printemps* like *Petrushka* has indeed several authors. Stravinsky has certainly not collaborated in it only as a musician, but also as a poet. He had a hand in the invention of the subject. One must not underestimate the importance of Roerich who for a long time now has been absorbed by a kind of prehistorical mysticism and whose style reappears in more than one choreographic pattern. But one must above all apologize to Nijinski. Our injustice to him has been such that we must long bear the shame of it. We did not understand anything about his mistakes. We thought they led nowhere; they seemed to have followed the truth, whereas they preceded it; we took them for arbitrary deformations of an already attained ideal, whereas they were the clumsy approximations of a new ideal. True, without intending to do so, he did everything to mislead us. For on two occasions, as a pretext for his dances, he chose atmospheric music, whereas he was precisely striving in his choreography to eliminate the equivalent of atmosphere. Still it was we who were wrong; it was up to us to guess. And since we have not been able to do it, in order to make up for an error, let us retrospectively admire the heroic stubbornness of this creator. Not an instant of doubt;

---

*This fusion of souls, is it not in part, as Jacques Copeau has remarked in these pages [*N.R.F.*], the subject of Dostoevsky's novels? (J.R.)

he went through his own blunders without flinching. Rarely has an inventor's soul been so fully and peacefully preoccupied with his own invention. All he needed was to set it right in front of him. To someone who before the première was asking him what the *Sacre du Printemps* was, he replied: "Oh! you will not like this either," and sketching with his arms the lateral and stilted gesture which we learned to know from the *Prélude à l'Après-midi d'un faune*[5], he added: "There will be some more of this!"

Indeed, there was "some more of this." Moreover, it was a masterpiece. I beg forgiveness for expressing at such length enthusiasm which is so strong without giving reasons for it. It is because they are too numerous and too important to be produced easily at once. The work is so new that in order to fully understand it, it is necessary to let time ripen and deepen the thoughts which it suggests. This work is epoch-making, not only in the history of dance and music, but in that of all the arts. Its beauty overflows on all sides. But that only makes it more difficult to encompass. That is why at this point I ask permission to pause and catch breath before I approach the *Sacre du Printemps* head on, and to postpone to a forthcoming issue the detailed explanation of its novelty. If I succeed in making clearer than I have been able to do at this time the reasons why I attach such a considerable importance to it, this will be my excuse for having several times undertaken to talk about a simple ballet.

NOTES

1 *Le Sacre du Printemps.* Ballet by Igor Stravinsky, Nicolas Roerich, Vaslav Nijinski: (Théâtre des Champs Elysées) *N.R.F., X* (August 1913), 309-13..

2 *Le Spectre de la Rose,* ballet after a poem by T. Gautier, adapted by J.-L. Vaudoyer. Music by C. M. von Weber, orchestration by H. Berlioz. Choreography by M. Fokine. Décor and costumes by L. Bakst. Première: Casino, Monte Carlo, April 19, 1911.

3 *Jeux.* Music by C. Debussy. Choreography by V. Nijinsky. Décor and costumes by L. Bakst. Première: Théâtre des Champs Elysées, Paris, May 15, 1913.

4 The initial reaction of the Paris public to *Le Sacre de Printemps* was extremely negative.

5 *L'Après-midi d'un faune*, ballet after the poem by Stéphane Mallarmé. Music by Claude Debussy. Choreography by Vaslav Nijinsky. Décor by Léon Bakst. Première: Théâtre du Châtelet, Paris, May 29, 1912.

Le Sacre du Printemps (II)[1]
by Jacques Rivière

The great novelty in the *Sacre du Printemps* is to do without "sauce." Here is a work which is absolutely pure. Acid and hard, if you wish; but no juice tarnishes its brightness, no culinary artistry alters or smudges its contours. It is not a "work of art" with all the usual little faking. Nothing is blurred, nothing is diminished by shadows; no veils or poetic softening; no trace of atmosphere. The work is whole and rough, its pieces remain raw; they are presented to us without being prepared to be digested; everything here is frank, intact, limpid, and unrefined.

The *Sacre du Printemps* is the first masterpiece that we could contrast with those of impressionism.

I

Let us first consider the music. It is stripped of all vibration, it has lost the halo we have become accustomed to see surrounding orchestral music.

Debussy's symphonic music is a fire from which vibrating rays escape; there is a nucleus and all around a vaporous shimmering, the wavering of a thousand indistinct harmonics; we are in the midst of the flight of sounds; they leave us and they disperse in all directions, forming around us a delicate haze which is ceaselessly vanishing. Such a music can express nothing but by allusion; it does not reach things; it merely points to them; it vaguely orients us to them; it stirs them without seizing them. Everything this music expresses remains outside it, merely kept in its environment; it encloses nothing, but there are a thousand indistinct presences which it annexes gently and persuades to remain near it. The pleasure which we enjoy on hearing it is precisely that of feeling ourselves drawn toward something, we do not quite know what, but which is quite near, which throbs and half slips away.

Without violence, without ingratitude but quite distinctly, Stravinsky frees himself from Debussyism. He has realized that this delightful halo, in the midst of which his master's music always appears drowned, ran the risk of merely becoming "sauce" in the work of a disciple. He deliberately removes all indecision, all wavering from his symphony. In an article on *Le Sacre du Printemps* which he published in *Montjoie*[2] among several naive pronouncements, which but enhances my trust, for they are typical of a true creator, I call attention to the following sentence: "From this melody (that of the Prelude) I have excluded the *strings* which with their crescendos and diminuendos can evoke and represent too well the human voice—and in the forefront I placed the *woodwinds* which are dryer, neater, less rich in facile expression, and, for this very reason, in my opinion moving." From the beginning, for whoever listened carefully and knew how to hear differences, Stravinsky's music gave out a flat and definite sound which was specifically its own. It did not spread, it did not abandon itself to its own resonance. In its *fireworks*, in its bouquets, there was something fixed, closed, and entirely determined. Its most dazzling passages did not even have the moistness of scintillation. The music seemed inspired by dryness as by a spring; it sprang, spread out, and fell again with a profusion at once vivid and dead. But this terseness and this contraction of sounds become especially striking in the *Sacre du Printemps*: one feels this from the first measures; there is no radiating, no flight; the melody progresses along a narrow path; it develops and lasts without the slightest effusion; we are seized by an all-powerful stifling; the sounds die without having overflowed the space they filled at birth; nothing escapes, nothing flies away, everything brings us back and overwhelms us. Never has anyone heard such magnificently circumscribed music.

This is not simply a negative novelty. Stravinsky did not merely divert himself by running counter to Debussy. If he has chosen instruments which do not quiver, which do not say anything more than what they say, whose timbre has no expansiveness and which are like abstract words, it is because he wants to state everything directly, expressly, by name. That is where his principal preoccupation lies. That is personal innovation in contemporary music. No more echo, because nothing must henceforth be expressed by simple allusion. In his chosen subject, he wants no detail to be attained by diffusion of sound waves alone, or to be only touched by the fringes of the orchestra. He eschews using shock tactics. He does not want to count on what the orchestration carries along in passing, by a chance and momentary adherence. Instead he turns to each thing and names it; he goes everywhere; he speaks wherever it is necessary and in the most exact, the narrowest, the most textual fashion. His voice identifies itself with the object, consumes it, replaces it; instead of evoking, it pronounces it. He leaves out nothing; on the contrary, he goes back to things: he finds them, seizes them, and brings them back. His movement does not consist in calling, nor in pointing to external regions, but in catching, holding, and scrutinizing. In this way, Stravinsky is bringing about brilliantly and with an unmatchable perfection the same revolution which is being accomplished more modestly and more painfully in literature: he goes from the sung to the spoken, from invocation to discourse, from poetry to recital.

All the characteristics of his music proceed from this will to use direct and textual expression.

Let us first consider its spaciousness. There is in it a kind of height and airiness; it is full of bold lacunae, of simplification, of broad cuts. As the musician always has several things to say at the same time and wants to say all of them right where they are, scattered as they are, his orchestration ceases to be a mass, a compact focus, dispensing its rays all around. He no longer is at the center like the poet, who without moving spreads himself in a flow of allusion; instead, like a general who briskly presses the enemy in its three or four strongest positions at once, he attacks the subject in all its essential points. As diverse as the directions to be followed may be, he follows them all at the same time without the least difficulty; he is actively ubiquitous and this enables him to move at the same time in several opposite directions. Thus one clearly perceives an indefinable distance and play between the different parts of his orchestration. One goes back and forth between these parts; each has its orientation; they come and go; they cross, meet, get caught on to each other; there are formidable collisions among them, but never any blending or fusion. They always remain well set apart and quite free. Take this bass-drum—it is left all by itself; its rustic gaiety is not spiced by a surreptitious accompaniment. Even if other instruments are speaking at the same moment, they are saying something else, they are elsewhere, and I am delighted as much at the feel of the clear and bold intervals of their simultaneous discourse as at hearing them. Everything comes at me at the same time, but not in a whiff, not like a complex and soft bunch of perfumes. It is a system of movements; they are distinct and determined voices.

Not only in harmony but the melody itself recaptures in Stravinsky a breadth, an ease, and if I dare say so, an altitude to which we were no longer accustomed. Indeed, since in Debussy melody only served to suggest sentiments, it hardly moved; it seemed crushed under the weight of the infinity in which it bathed; it crawled flat, and almost without changing level, by means of small and exquisite inflections rising or lowering by half a tone, it indicated things. But Stravinsky wants to say them, to state them quite explicitly; thus his phrase rises until it equals them; it develops boldly, it rises in tiers. In his work, melody has as it were an intimate ascending force; it nibbles at elevation with admirable ease and it absorbs it in great bites. It is as if the melody allowed the space which until then had been weighting it down to penetrate it. Nothing is more moving for me than its strides. Melody has lost the aristocratic timidity and reserve which were beginning to make me impatient; it no longer remains half-way uphill, it no longer maneuvres with an unerring but ultimately tiresome refinement, between the too natural, too square, too exact forms into which it could fall. It falls there first off, deliberately and with confidence. Say it is coarse, if you like; but to surrender to a coarseness so pure, requires just a crumb more of genius than to avoid it carefully. I recognize Stravinsky's genius best in the way in which he faces banality. He does not attempt to escape it; instead, when he encounters it, he accepts it, he speaks in its voice, he uses all its advantages, he goes along with it as far as it wishes to lead him, and almost without touching anything, by the very ease which he keeps in its company, he transfigures it, he elevates it to the level of the sublime. It is this ability to expose himself, to become involved without fear in what is ordinary and facile, which gives his melody its tranquility, its breadth, its spaciousness. O! how I love its clean, familiar backward and forward motion, its way of touching down with its feet wherever necessary so that the feeling may be exactly run through, the thing expressed as it ought to be! I am thinking of the trumpet air of the Ballerina in *Petrushka* and of the phrase—so limpid, so straight, so unperturbed in its crossing back and forth of the entire orchestra—which underlines, in the first tableau of the *Sacre*, the lateral glides of the Adolescents in red.

The desire to express everything down to the last detail explains a second characteristic of Stravinsky's music: its acrobatic character, which some have pretended to regard as an effect of the musician's virtuosity. It would take some affectation to insist on ignoring the unusual and almost extravagant aspects of this music. It bursts out constantly at improbable and theoretically inaccessible points. Just as Petrushka, killed by the Black Man, all of a sudden reappears at the top of the canvas booth, it also pops out at every moment where without a miracle it really has no right to show itself. Nothing stops it; it has a formidable kind of ease; every obstacle gives in to it right away; it does not try to go around it, instead it moves forward and everything is straightened out under its steps; before one has had time to understand, it has gone by. It continuously moves in the realm of the extraordinary; and only there does it find itself at ease; it constantly advances on a cliffroad; but this is a highway for it. It is certainly natural that before treating any other subject, Stravinsky should have chosen to write a fairy-tale. His music is a tissue of magical tricks and feats. I see him in the midst of his work as an almighty enchanter amid his court of slaves. All he needs is an idea: as strange, as capricious as it may be, such as Koschei's[3] ferocious henchmen subdued by the Firebird, sounds rush forth, jostle and crush each other, but follow this idea. It has to work; there is constantly an "in-spite-of-everything" element in this music; like children pulled by the hand, the instruments come up askew and panting; they perform their part only by becoming distorted and surpassing themselves; they are seized by the sovereign attraction of the idea and they advance in the attitude in which they were surprised, without having had the time to find their normal balance. Everything occurs as in a supernatural world where the power of mind over matter suddenly becomes infinite. What could be more anomalous, more incomprehensible and more perfect than at the end of the first tableau of *Le Sacre du Printemps*, during the Adolescents' circular race, that music, in which there no longer is melody, harmony, or play of timbres, but only a kind of buzzing of the rhythm, of pure animation, of abstract whirlwind, maintained and prolonged by the monotony of terror itself?

All of Stravinsky's music is a fabric of such prodigies. But one must see well the meaning of this. These are not ordinary acrobatics but simple accomplishments of craftsmanship. On the contrary, they are possible only because their author has not put his craft first. He sees only what he has to say; he applied himself wholly to it, he loses, he forgets himself in it; and it is from this dedication to the object that his irresistible and enchanting power is born; one is always rewarded for having had faith; the object, when we no longer see anything else, difficult though it may appear, always ends up inventing within us that which is necessary to express it and to manifest it for all to see. I am therefore saying that the peculiarities continuously used by Stravinsky are not there for us to admire or to be astonished by, but on the contrary to put us in direct contact, in immediate communication with admirable and astonishing things. They are not intended to make us think about a surmounted difficulty, but come to do away with a difficulty which was in our path. These peculiarities do not strive to create in our mind a distance to traverse, but to eliminate one, to bring closer to us that which we would have reached only through effort. Instead of soliciting our wonder, they strive to introduce us quickly into the marvelous and to set us at ease with it. Their strangeness comes from the fact that they take upon themselves all that is impossible, inaccessible, revolting in the things which they want to express; they absorb all their mystery in order to remove it for us. Almost from beginning to end of *Le Sacre du Printemps* the metrical indications change for each measure; this anomaly, apparently so unwarranted, is there only so that we always remain in accord with the sentiment expressed, so that its rhythm may be ours, so that we spontaneously find ourselves in step. Here we recognize again Stravinsky's essential principle, that of expressing everything textually. For him there is nothing which should not be tackled head-on: the object may be fantastic and a thousand leagues away from us, we must go and find it, we must discover the entrance and enter into it the right way; he takes charge of the whole voyage, and like the flying horse, in an

72

instant drops us off at the threshold. It has been said that it is an eccentric music. Yes, but one must take the word literally: it is a music which has given up the center in order to always present itself normally before the most out-of-the-way paths, a music which has extravagant gusts, but so as to blow straight ahead. Thus, when it rises, what after all is its most surprising aspect, what grips us about it from the beginning, is the feeling of ease with which everything it tells presents itself to the mind.

For I must return to it as I am ending: its greatest beauty is its directness. It speaks; all one has to do is listen; it comes, it springs, it gushes out, and it leaves us nothing to do but be there. It unfolds its narrative like a grandmother:

> A spider,
> Had tied me by the wrist with a thread and I was in
> grass up to my neck;
> And from the middle of its web, it was telling me
> stories like a woman sitting down.[4]

Words whose naiveté no strangeness can tire. We think that this bundle of peculiar timbres will be content to entertain us with its fantasy; but here it is blending into a single song. This big, complex, and clumsy thing, about which we wonder if it will even be able to move, suddenly starts off with a single motion; it advances, it comes near, it reveals a kind of voice, and it addresses us, explains its business, pours out its trust; it develops an eloquence—an eloquence which right away becomes very close and intimate, quite pressing and attached to us. We have already forgotten its anomalous composition: we are quiet, we are awaiting what follows; we are held in suspense by this prodigious language whose every word is being forged anew and which yet is understandable at once. It is a joy to understand, a joy to receive news, a joy to be "put wise." The extraordinary story is transmitted to us; we take it in in big and easy morsels; as to savages sitting in a circle, the eldest of the tribe recites, as if it were evident, the supernatural adventures of the gods, so we listen to so many enormous fictions as they enter into our ears. Stravinsky is first and foremost the one who speaks, the teller. Thereby, in spite of the difference in their craft, he alone among all Russian musicians resembles Mussorgsky. It has not yet been sufficiently noticed how little Persian he is.[5] There is nothing exotic about him; no Almahs in his music; no picturesqueness whatsoewer. Even in *Firebird*, whose subject was conducive to a big production, there is not one measure that is simply descriptive; nothing which is not first of all intended to be true. Stravinsky's music is first of all a voice; that of the *niania*[6] which is urged on by an inexhaustible abundance which at times hurries and at other times tarries, stops and starts again, constantly trying the always-broken thread of her tale, knowing how to enhance it in no other way than by adding new episodes to it. Even lost in the history of monstrous times, it is still our mother Russia speaking to us and dispensing to us the treasures of her immemorial innocence.

II

As new as the music in the *Sacre du Printemps* may be, the fact that we have been able to compare it with that of Mussorgsky shows nevertheless that it has some affinities with what we are accustomed to and that we can trace its filiation approximately. The same is not true of the choreography, which no longer has any ties whatsoever with classical dance. Everything in it is started anew right on the spot, everything is re-invented. Its novelty is so brutal and so raw that the public should not be denied the right to rear before it, which, as a matter of fact, it did all too conscientiously.[7] Let us strive to define this novelty with some precision, in the timid hope of acclimating the public to it.

It is still, as I see it, doing without "sauce."

In general, in dance, thare are two kinds of "sauce," one might say. First, the Loïe Fuller[8] kind: plays of light, waving of draperies, wrapping of the body in veils which annul its bounds, a blurring of all the contours: the dancer tries first of all to lose herself in the surroundings, to drown herself in movements vaster and less defined, to hide all precise form in a kind of multicolored effusion of which she is but the indistinct and mysterious center. It is quite natural that Loïe Fuller should have been led to illustrate Debussy's *Nuages.*

From the beginning, the Russians have come out openly against this first kind of sauce. They made the body reappear under the veils, they brought it out of the undulating atmosphere in which it bathed and desired to move us only by its own movement and by the quite visible, quite evident figure which the dancer draws with his arms and with his legs. They have brought clarity back to dance. I remember the first evenings! It was for me the revelation of a new world. So it was possible to let all one's movements be visible, to trace them along without mystery, and yet be profound and pathetic, and to hold the spectators focused on oneself in suspense as if they had been watching the most confusing and the most enigmatic games. My discovery in art was analogous to that of geometry and science, and the joy I felt was the same as the satisfaction given by the perfect proof. With each of Nijinski's whirls made at the moment when, by kneeling and crossing his hands he would come to close the loop he had opened by leaping into space, all my pleasure was in visualizing again in thought the entire figure made by his movement. It was living, pure, strict, done with a dash and as if torn by force in one pull from the indecisive mass of the possible. No doubt whatever, no smudge, nothing to arouse hesitation in me; instead I was strong and happy as a man who in one glimpse sees a system of propositions which is scrupulously isolated from error in all its points.

Yet in this dance which seemed so rigorous to us, well before we realized it ourselves, Nijinski was able to discover that there still was another kind of "sauce," and he undertook to purge the choreography of this sauce completely. By a sort of malaise he felt in executing certain of Fokine's creations, he realized that there still was some play, a wavering, an internal vagueness which had to be reduced at all cost. This clarity could be refined, this exactness could be carried farther....From then on he knew no rest until he himself had given a turn of the screw, before he had tightened the bolts, so that the choreographic machine could attain its tightest functioning. He will be understood by those whom nothing in the world bothers more than the feeling of laxity and approximation.

Let us first determine what this second kind of sauce consists of. What is there that still envelops the dancer when he has rid himself of his props?

His upward leap, his passage, his flight through time, the arabesque he traces as he moves: "He travels on a path which he destroys as he moves along it; he follows a mysterious thread which becomes invisible behind him; with his gesture of dismissal, with these hands which he moves in the air, with this body which turns gently a thousand times, he seems like a magician busy trying to erase his tracks; we will not catch him; we will not succeed in holding him, in putting our arms on our hips in order to look at him at leisure from head to toe."[9] Something comes between him and us, and it is his very movement; we see him go by in a world parallel to ours but different from it; he is lost in his own voyage and we only see him through a mist formed by all his gestures and his implacable coming and going. Let us be more precise: with the first ten steps he takes, the dancer *traces* a line which immediately tends to leave him, to escape, to flee all alone, as a melody, when one has found its first ten notes, continues of itself, is improvised in a vacuum and ends up by imposing itself on the voice which gave it birth. There is a spring in it which pushes it away from its base. Once the first movements are invented by the body, it is as if, gaining consciousness, they should say to their author: "Enough now! Leave us on our own!" And there they are, unleashing themselves; by repetition, by doubling, by variation, they create each other, they bring out of themselves an infinite abundance.

The body which first dictated them, has become now merely a support; it now has only to receive and execute them. And so in their hands it loses its proper shape and articulation. They fix it, they correct it, they touch it up; they replace a hiatus in it by a passage: they reunite its members with a slender and continuous line; they erase angles, fill holes, throw bridges. From head to toe the body takes on a certain roundness and fluidity. An additional, an adventitious elegance descends upon it and becomes set. Like a well-made-up actor, it is no longer recognizable. The *Spectre de la Rose* offers the best example of this transfiguration. In it, Nijinski's body literally disappears in its own dance. Of this being, who is so muscular, whose features are so strong, so marked, one sees only exquisitely fleeting contours, only forms which are ceaselessly evanescent. Instead of being immersed in a colored atmosphere, he is in a dynamic one. But he receives from it almost as much imprecisions as Loïe Fuller from her luminous veils. Delightful as the spectacle may be, there is in the *Spectre de la Rose* a certain internal lack of truth by which I can no longer help being bothered.

The novelty of the *Sacre du Printemps* is doing without this dynamic sauce, returning to the body, the effort to keep closer to its natural movements so as to respond only to its most immediate, its most radical, its most etymological indications. In it movement is reduced to obedience; it is ceaselessly brought back to the body, tied to it, caught and pulled backward by it, like someone who is held by the elbow and thus prevented from fleeing. It is movement which does not go off by itself, which has been forbidden to sing its little ditty, it is movement which in every minute comes back to the body to take orders. In the body at rest there are a thousand latent directions, a whole system of lines through which it inclines toward the dance. Fokine made them meet in one movement which connected and drained all of them; he listened to them as a whole rather than to each alone; he expressed them by substitution, by replacing their diverging multitude by a simple and continuous arabesque. On the other hand, in the *Sacre du Printemps*, the movement is interrupted and started again as often as the body affords tendencies and opportunities; the dancer starts his flight as often as he feels points of departure in him. He recovers himself at every moment like a spring whose every trickle has to be exhausted one after the other; he goes back within himself and his dance becomes an analysis, a counting up of all the inclinations to move which he finds in it. Here we catch in Nijinski the same preoccupation as in Stravinsky: to approach each and every thing according to its proper orientation. Whatever the gap between them, he wants to follow straight out all the inclinations of the body and to come down to the movement with them alone. But since he cannot accompany all of them at the same time, as soon as he has followed one of them for an instant, he abruptly leaves it, he breaks away from it and goes back to look for another. The dance is both faithful and truncated. It is the same as our body; all the movements of which it is composed remain perfectly identical to the limbs which execute them; they have the same meaning and keep the same brevity; they remain joined to them and as if organically tied. And when one sees the dancer again in one's memory, instead of becoming erased behind his movements, he appears quite distinctly in their midst, in the same way as a Hindu god in the midst of his bristling arms.

In the way in which Nijinski has treated group movements, one finds the same effort to grasp detail, to discover and bring out individual injunctions. In Fokine's ballets, groups of dancers balanced each other exactly on each side of the stage; it was not the ridiculous symmetry of the Opera; but there was a regular distribution of masses, an equilibrium between them which the eye had to look for only long enough to have the pleasure of discovering it. It was not only a static equilibrium; it persisted in the dance, however tangled it might have been; a certain balancing subsisted in the very heart of tumult. Every figure was conceived after the pattern of an exchange or of a to-and-fro motion: once the dancers had taken hold of a motion, they would throw it to each other back and forth endlessly like a ball. One group would never make a movement but in response to a movement of the opposite group; its forward and backward movements, its flights or its returns were only intended as compensation. Consequently one's attention was soon diverted from it; the group disappeared in its dialogue with the others and one could no longer see anything but the choreographic motif of which it was a part; on the stage there no longer was anything but a certain form of agitation, a pure mode of movement. And since such a figure was too abstract to be renewed indefinitely in its essence, soon Fokine was no longer able to show his invention except by modifying its pretext and the props. It was to no purpose that he substituted the golden fruits which the tsarinas threw to each other in *Firebird* for the daggers in *Thamar* and the pikes in *Daphnis et Chloé*; he was struggling against the impossible. In order to recapture the source of variety, it would have been necessary first to go back to detail, reestablish contact with individual aspects.

This is what Nijinski so well realized. He has approached each individual group; he has observed its indications and its tendencies like a scientist; he has seen it rise, shiver, undulate, be carried off abruptly by its inner force; he has followed its molecular formation, he has caught its instincts at the moment they declared themselves, he has made himself the spectator and the historian of its least initiatives. The dance of each group consists of movements that it has been hatching while separated from all the others--like the spontaneous combustion that occurs in haystacks. There is in all the choreography of the *Sacre du Printemps* a profound asymmetry which is part of the essence of the work. Each group begins by itself; it does not make any motion that is inspired by the need to answer, to compensate, to reestablish the equilibrium; off to one side, it stirs and sets out, it glides to the side and draws our attention after it. In the end we do recapture it, but it is because another group has caught it and is taking it away. There is no lack of composition; on the contrary, there is one and of the subtlest kind, in the encounters, the comings face-to-face with each other, the minglings, the combats of these strange battalions. But this composition does not precede detail; it does not command it; it makes of its diversity the best it can. The impression of unity which we do not, for an instant, cease to feel is of the kind one feels when seeing the inhabitants of the same world going about, meeting, mingling with one another, separating, according to their individual purposes, at the same time familiar and forgetful of each other.

We have just examined in what sense Nijinski has reacted against Fokine, what he has refused, what he has destroyed. We must now understand the positive aspect of his innovation. How has he benefited from this doing away with the "sauce?" For what purpose has he interrupted the movement and broken up the choreographic ensembles? What beauty is hidden in this reduced and skimpy dance? Without taking into account at this point its marvelous appropriateness as applied to the *Sacre du Printemps*, it seems easy for me to see in what way it surpasses Fokine's dance.

The latter is fundamentally inappropriate for the expression of sentiments; one can see in it only a vague joy, merely physical and faceless. Indeed in its liquid and continuous movement, as in the great arabesques of Renaissance painters, the expressive power of motion, its secret, its inner force dissolve and become diluted. On the indefinite road on which the dancer sets out, they find too easy an outlet and they scatter in vain. Instead of being the object that the movement strives to paint and make visible, the sentiment is no longer anything but the pretext which unleashes it, and it is quite soon forgotten in the abundance of which it is the source; it is soon lost in the repetitions which it brings about. The body carries everything; its freedom reaches even the soul, and destroys its secret places, its resources, its reserves.

By breaking up movement, by bringing it back to a simple motion, Nijinski returned expression to dance. All the angles, all the breaks in his choreography prevent sentiment from escaping. Movement closes on it, stops it, contains it; by its perpetual changing of direction, he takes all outlets away from it; he imprisons it by his very brevity. The body is no longer a way through which the soul can escape; on the contrary, it gathers itself together around it; it represses its thrust, and by the very effort which it exerts against the soul, it becomes completely impregnated with it and pulls it outside. From the constraint which it imposes on the soul, the body receives something spiritual which I cannot describe but which appears in all its aspects. There is something profound and tight in this fettered dance. All that it loses in liveliness, in dash, in capriciousness, it gains in meaning.

Fokine's dance was so lacking in expression that, in order to communicate to the spectators the changes in their souls, the actors had to resort to a facial mimesis by frowning or smiling. This was added to their motions, was superimposed on them, and by this very fact signified their powerlessness. It was a reinforcement which was brought up, a resource of another order which relieved the indigence of the choreographic language proper.

Instead, in Nijinski's dance the face does not now play an independent role; it extends the body; it is merely its flower. It is first the body itself that speaks. It moves only as a whole, it forms a block, and its language consists of sudden leaps with its arms and legs outstretched, or in going to the side with knees bent and head fallen on the shoulder. At first sight it seems less adroit, less varied, less intelligent. Yet, with its compact moves, its brusque about-faces, its ways of stopping short and then frantically shaking on the spot, it says a thousand times more than a fluent, quick, and elegant conversionalist animated by Fokine. Nijinski's language is perpetually attentive to detail; it does not let anything go by; it enters into every corner. There is no turn of phrase, no pirouette, no preterition. The dancer is no longer carried away by a light and indifferent inspiration. Instead of brushing by them in his flight, he falls back on things with all his weight, he leaves a mark on each with his heavy and total fall. On each sentiment he encounters and wants to express, he takes a standing jump; with an abrupt leap, he turns toward it, covers it, and keeps on imitating it for an instant. He forgets everything in order to become like it for a time; he smothers it for a time with his shape, he blinds it with his entire being. Since he does not have to put any connection between his successive motions or to think constantly about what follows, he does not withhold anything of himself for the transitions. He gives in completely to the invitation of the inner object, he becomes unique like it, he names it with the momentary inertia of his entire body. Let us remember Nijinski as a dancer. With what eloquence he used to arch himself like a cat around sentiments! How closely he brooded over them! How well he knew how to arrange all his limbs in their image and find within himself their faithful effigy! All he breaks in the dance, all he strips it of, is in order to reach a material, a full and opaque imitation of emotions. He takes his dancers, he arranges their arms, he shapes them, he would break them if he dared; he works those bodies with a pitiless brutality as if they were things; he imposes upon them impossible movements and attitudes which seem deformed. But this is in order to wring from them all the expressiveness they can give. And indeed, in the end they speak. From all these strange and constrained forms arises a kind of certainty; they distinctly represent a thousand difficult and secret objects at which one has only to look.

Yes, this is clear and easy; it has taken the very contours of that which has to be understood. Here is the sentiment indicated, fixed, presented before us. It is there like a big puppet that the dancer leaves behind while he goes on. There is nothing more moving than this physical image of the soul's passions. It is quite different from their expression through articulated language. Not that it goes to greater depth, but there is a notation of details and finesse in them, which language could not attain. But through this physical attitude we are led closer to our passions, we are placed in their presence in a more immediate way, we contemplate them before we can articulate them, before a throng of words bustles around them, countless and full of nuances, but loquacious. There is no need to translate; this is not a symbol from which it should be necessary to go on to the thing. But while our intelligence is in the dark, we watch; we are present with our body, and it is our body which understands, through a certain disposition, a certain inner cognizance....Every motion by the dancer is as it were a word which would resemble me. If it sometimes appears strange, it is so only in the eyes of my thought; for right away it meets with my limbs, with the depths of my organism in a low, full, and perfect harmony. Just as the music introduced its story to us "in large easy pieces," so it is that we look at this extravagant dance with a sort of gross credulity and in an intimacy which "goes beyond words." We are in front of it like children at a Guignol show: they do not need any explanation; but they laugh, they tremble, they understand as the show goes along.

Nijinski has given the dance a power to convey meaning of which it was deprived. But did his diligence in relating it to the body, in confusing it with the narrow solidity of our limbs, not risk depriving it of its bloom and of its grace? And indeed, where is the grace of these petty, clumsy motions which are always captive, always being brutally interrupted as soon as they are about to gain momentum? It seems that in the choreography of the *Sacre du Printemps* there is some cacophony.

Yet grace is not in roundness; it is not imcompatible with an angular design. There is a grace here, I claim, and a deeper one than that of the *Spectre de la Rose* because it is better integrated. Grace is not something independent; it does not alight from above on things like a bird; it is only the outward emanation of an exact necessity, only the effect of an impeccable inner adjustment. Now, in the choreography of the *Sacre du Printemps*, everything is set with the greatest rigor; in order to create motions such as we see him composing them, Nijinski cultivated and developed them for a long time; he chose them in the midst of the confused and diverse ramifications of our instinctive movements, he preserved them against the others, he pushed slightly and led them a little farther away from the body than they would have gone of themselves. In a word, he patiently returned them to their unique perfection. And from this perfecting process is born an unknown harmony. If one is willing to cease confusing grace with symmetry and arabesque, one will find it in every page of the *Sacre du Printemps*, in those faces seen in profile upon shoulders viewed from the front, in those elbows clamped to the body, in those horizontal forearms, in those open and rigid hands, in this trembling which comes down like a wave from the head to the feet of the dancers, in the obscure, scattered, preoccupied promenade of the Adolescents in the Second Tableau. One will even find it again in the dance of the Chosen Maiden, in the short and abortive starts which agitate her, in her clumsiness, in her horrible moments of waiting, in her captive and distorted gait, as well as in that arm raised to the sky which she holds straight above her head as a sign of appeal, of threat and of protection.

III

Throughout the analysis which I have just sketched of the *Sacre du Printemps*, I have considered the means used by Stravinsky and by Nijinski as if these techniques had value in themselves, independently from the subject to which they are applied. This separation may seem artificial and I may be criticized for having seen a whole new technique in something which has been invented and has meaning only for a well-defined work. This choreography, in its angularity, some will tell me, is only for the purpose of representing the still shapeless and awkward gesticulation of primitive beings. This music, which is so stifled, is only to paint the dense anguish of spring. Both strictly serve the chosen theme; they do not go beyond it, they do not let themselves be distinguished from it.

I will answer that the distinctive feature of masterpieces is precisely to create for their own use an expression which is so complete, so skillful and new that it quite naturally becomes a generally used technique. Nothing good is invented separately. In order to have ideas which are new and somewhat far-reaching, it is necessary to work on something quite precise; one must want to express something in such a way that it cannot be confused with anything else. It is while one strives toward something individual, while one gathers all the faculties of one's mind toward the same small point, that suddenly, as if under excessive pressure, really wide-ranging inventions burst forth. It is from extreme urgency that true fecundity is born. Because Stravinsky and Nijinski meant only to solve a specific problem, they happen to have discovered a general solution. And if in an attempt analogous to theirs the Cubists have failed until now, it is because they first elaborated a solution in the abstract which, intact and absurd, they tried to place in their works only afterward.

To these considerations one must add that *Petrushka* already contained the germ of the choreography of the *Sacre du Printemps*. Although his name appeared only once on the billboard, it is certain that Nijinski collaborated in the first as well as the second of these works. We recognize his style in the dance which the three puppets do in one spot, and the pathetic scene where Petrouchka is imprisoned. One finds the same technique of connecting the movements to the body, the same use of the jerk, the same ceaseless concern to preserve all the expressive force of the movement. And at the same time, this fixed idea appeared marvelously right, suitable, and appropriate. Already then we could not imagine that it could work for another subject. Yet what a difference between the theme of *Petrushka* and that of the *Sacre!* How can the means which have so pertinently served both the one and the other be denied a general bearing, and why should it be forbidden to consider them outside their original use?

However, the moment has come for us to consider nothing else but the *Sacre du Printemps*, to place ourselves squarely in front of this terrible work, to lock ourselves up with it in order to experience the special commotion it is intended to cause within us.

Let us ask ourselves what it represents. What do we have here before our eyes? What is happening here? The work is so rich that we can discover in it two levels of meaning. First it has an evident, official, avowed meaning. The *Sacre du Printemps* is a sociological ballet. It is the extraordinary vision of an age which until now we have had to painfully reconstruct with the help of scientific documents and which now has been made perceptible to our imagination.

> "Indeed ancient humanity had come to meet its sister,
> And as formerly on the day of parting, we were looking
> at each other on an equal footing."[10]

We are watching man's movements at a time when he did not yet exist as an individual. Creatures still hold together; they go in groups, in colonies, in schools; they are caught in the horrible indifference of society; they are devoted to the god they together form and from whom they have not yet been able to disentangle themselves. Nothing individual appears in their faces. At no moment of her dance does the chosen maiden betray the personal terror with which her soul should be filled. She is accomplishing a rite, she is absorbed by a social function, and without giving any sign of comprehension or interpretation, she moves according to the will and the pulls of a being vaster than she, a monster full of ignorance and lusts, cruelty, and darkness. It is Moloch brought back from the depths of the oldest epochs. He stirs, he opens his maw before us. A base and mindless god! His altars are made in his likeness: they are those stones standing at the crossings of the shapeless plain, those animal skulls on pikes. He is a god who weighs down at head level like the brazen sky! A god who reigns on all fours, and devours his children as a cow would graze! Man is dominated by what is most inert, opaque, and limited in him: his life with others.

But there is in the *Sacre du Printemps* something even more serious, a second meaning, more secret and more hideous. This ballet is a biological ballet. It is not only the dance of the most primitive man: it is dance *before* man. In his article in *Montjoie*, Stravinsky states that he wanted to show us the rise of spring. But it is not the spring to which poets have accustomed us, with its quiverings, its music, its tender sky, and its pale greenery. No, nothing but the harshness of the vital impetus, nothing but the "panic"[11] terror which accompanies the rise of the sap, nothing but the horrible work of the cells. It is spring seen from within, spring in its effort, in its spasm, in its dividing process. It is as if one were watching a drama of the microscope; it is the story of cellular fission, the deep task whereby the nucleus separates itself from itself and reproduces itself; it is the dividing process of birth; these are scissions and recurrences of matter restless down to its very substance; these are broad circling heaps of protoplasm, germinating plates, zones, circles, placentas. We are plunged into the lower realms; we are watching dull movements, stupid comings and goings, all the fortuitous whirlwinds whereby matter slowly rises to life. There never was a more beautiful illustration for mechanist theories. There is something profoundly blind in this dance. An enormous question is posed by all these beings which stir before our eyes. It is no different from them. They carry it about with them without understanding it, like an animal which goes around in its cage and does not tire of coming and touching the bars with its forehead. They have no other organ but their organism as a whole, and it is with it that they search. They go here and there and stop; they rush forward as a parcel and wait. There is nothing ahead of them that they must catch up with. No ideal to regain. One is always farthest along by remaining with them. As the blood, which, without any other motive but its pressure, comes from within and knocks against the walls of the skull, they ask for egress and advent. And little by little through the brutal patience and obstinacy of their questioning, a sort of solution forms which in itself is not different from them either, which also becomes confused with the mass of their body, and which is life.

On the evening of the premiere of the *Sacre du Printemps*, there were, with me, like dregs at the bottom of my immense admiration, a certain sadness and depression. My heart was weighed down by the heaviness of physical things, by a mineral inertia. For the first time I felt that evolutionist theories were despairingly possible. I discovered in myself the traces of a wretched and crawling state; I was taken over again by primeval narrowness; it seemed to me that I had been born one day from this *anguish* of which I had just seen the prodigious representation. Ah! how far I was from humanity! How its voice was becoming weak and distant to my ears! There are works which are swollen with complaints, hopes, encouragements. One finds in them cause for suffering, for regret, for being confident; they contain all the beautiful stirrings of the soul; one surrenders to them as one listens to the advice of a friend; there is something moral about them and they always have something in common with pity. But the *Sacre du Printemps* is a piece of the primitive globe which has been preserved without aging and which continues to breathe mysteriously before our eyes with its inhabitants and its flora. It is a wreck from the past, teeming, and gnawed through and through by a familiar and monstrous life. It is a rock full of dens out of which emerge unknown creatures busy with tasks long since indecipherable and outmoded.

NOTES

1 *"Le Sacre du Printemps,"* *N.R.F., X* (November 1913), 706-30.

2 *Montjoie* VIII, May 29, 1913. [J.R.].

3 "Koschei the Deathless" is the enchanter whom Ivan Tsarevich overcomes at the end of the ballet.

4   Paul Claudel: *L'Echange*, dans *L'Arbre*, p. 170. [J.R.].

5   Because of Rimsky and Balakirev, and also because of ballets such as *Scheherazade* and *Thamar*, we have ended up confusing Russia and Persia. I think there are a few little differences anyway between these two countries.
If he saw some inhabitant of Teheran walking in Russia, the average Russian would perhaps ask himself with the same amazement as Montesquieu's Frenchmen: "How can one be a Persian?" Let us go a step further: I imagine that *Scheherezade* and *Thamar* must not resemble the true Persia much more than *Carmen* the true Spain. [J.R.].

6   The nanny.

7   Rivière is alluding to the initially violent negative reaction of the public to the *Sacre du Printemps.*

8   Loïe Fuller (1862-1928) was an American dancer. Inventor of serpentine dance (about 1890); she danced and later headed a school of dancing in Paris.

9   This passage is taken from an article I wrote last year (July 1, 1912) on Fokine and in which I advanced more than one assertion which today Nijinski forces me not quite to repudiate, but to go beyond--as he himself surpassed Fokine without repudiating him. [J.R.].

10   Paul Claudel: *Tête d'Or*, in *l'Arbre*, p. 131 [J.R.].

11   Rivière used the word in its etymological sense; i.e., a terror inspired by Pan, the primeval nature god of the Greeks.

The Russian Season: *The Nightingale*, opera in three tableaux by
Igor Stravinsky, based on a tale by Andersen.
    The Golden Cockerel, opera in three tableaux by Rimsky-Korsakov.
    The Legend of Joseph, ballet in one act by Richard Strauss based on a
libretto by Hugo von Hoffmannsthal and by Count Harry Kessler (at
the *Opéra)*[1]

by Jacques Rivière

A rather strange adventure is happening to Stravinsky. After having
written a work which was the magnificent realization of a theory of
esthetics until then embryonic and confused, here he is writing another
work to demonstrate this theory of esthetics, and to demonstrate it
word for word, minutely, nigglingly, with a diligence which reminds one
of the school-boyish and necessitous fashion with which it was expressed before him. He makes me think of a general who has completely forgotten that he has just won a great victory and is making the most ela-
borate, the most detailed arrangements, entirely lacking in genius, in
order to gain advantage over a vanished enemy. In reality, we are, I believe, before a case of a recognition phenomenon, but a recognition
which I cannot help but find most untimely. It is indisputable that some
of the principles on which the *Sacre du Printemps* was based had first
been sketched by the Cubists and the Futurists. Stravinsky seems to
have noticed this after the fact and, quite alarmed by this coincidence
which the unity of tendencies within the same generation is sufficient to
explain, believed he had to go back toward these impotent precursors,
to listen to their petty advice, accept their petty axioms, collect their
petty discoveries and, in order to thank them, write *The Nightingale*.
This is too much abnegation! It is the gentlemen Futurists that it be-
hooves to catch up with Stravinsky, if they can, not Stravinsky to wait
for them.
Does this mean that *The Nightingale*[2] is worth no more than the elu-
cubrations of Marinetti's disciples? It would be a shame to let anyone
believe it, even if only for an instant. An artist of Stravinsky's class will
never succeed in lowering himself so much, even if he works at it; even
if he persists in making himself mediocre, he can only pretend to be so.
In *The Nightingale*, genius reappears at all the seams, like water in a
saturated soil; the work is full of incomparable finds. It is nonetheless
true that in its essence it is similar to cubist and futurist works: first, like
them, it insists above all on its intentions, it shows outwardly the principles which should be hidden in its foundations, it asserts what it wants
to be instead of allowing to appear what it is. Furthermore, these inten-

tions and these principles are those of the strictest cubism, of the most orthodox futurism.

We find a clue in the manner in which he wrote it that Stravinsky wished to make a demonstration of *The Nightingale*. He began to compose it about 1909; but after having finished the first act, he abandoned the work; it is only this year that he picked it up again and finished it. Subject abandoned. I am afraid that here it may mean: a subject which did not impose itself with sufficient exigency on the musician's mind. A subject picked up again would then mean a subject in which the musician has seen afterwards, at a moment when he had ceased completely to be subjected to its attraction, a means of making his new preoccupations known, a vehicle for the discoveries of a technical order which he thought he had made in the interval. Whatever the significance of these inductions, it is evident in any case that the subject here is indifferent to the author. It remains passive in the midst of his imagination, it shows no pretention, it does not attempt to gain recognition and be accepted for itself. We are quite far away here from the particular, autonomous, appelative pressure, from the narrow and fixed appeal that the *Sacre du Printemps* must have exerted on Stravinsky! *The Nightingale* remains inert in his hand. And indeed, Andersen's tale has "demanded so little" that it has become almost unrecognizable; in the musician's translation, I find neither his winged naïveté, nor his nice irony; it is treated with the same casual despotism that Nijinski formerly showed toward Debussy's music.

To tell the truth, it is not really for having mangled Andersen's tale that I blame Stravinsky. It happens rather often that a great artist notices in a predecessor's work that is already known, well defined, and explored a new subject half set in its contours and yet different from it, like some monstrous parasite. Is it not in this fashion, for example, that Wagner perceived the *Tristan Romance* and extracted from it his *Tristan and Isolde*? Andersen's tale could have very well harbored for Stravinsky a new subject which might have been awaiting him as its liberator and which, barely untangled from its bonds, would have jumped on him. An indeed, in two or three places in *The Nightingale* one finds traces of a work as black, horrible, and petty as the bowels of China! Had the work developed and blossomed, we would have quite easily accepted the unfaithfulness done to the tale. But it remains in the state of a mere potential.

Yet, even without having discovered a new subject in Andersen's tale, Stravinsky still had the right, in a pinch, to transform it if it had been to satisfy the needs of a personal search, for his own edification, in order to establish a technical point which remained obscure in his own eyes. I hold absolutely nothing against Nijinski for his two *coups d'état* against Debussy's music; at the time when he perpetrated them, he was in the midst of a period of experimentation; he was working on the mastery of a new choreographic manner; he was in the difficult situation of one who is trying to find and can see nothing but tools in everything that comes to hand. His decision to ignore the suggestions of the music and to build his ballet apart from it, so to speak, was a heroic act of renunciation of immediate success in order to make a higher success possible in the future. But Stravinsky is in an entirely different situation: at the moment when he writes *The Nightingale*, he is in full possesion of his own manner; he has already carried it to its perfection. The authority he assumes with respect to his subject is therefore quite arbitrary; he was inspired only by the pleasure of showing pure form, and as it were in a vacuum, the techniques which he has mastered and which he advocates. What I expressly reproach him for is to have considered his subject not as a means of instructing himself but of instructing us, as a pulpit from which to read us his lecture. The lecture is, of course, the most subtle, the most elegant and refined that one can imagine (and one even sees the professor smiling at the thought that most will not understand anything of it). It is a lecture nevertheless. *The Nightingale* is written against the public, which amounts to a way of being written for the public. Three were involved at the moment when the work was being created; in addition to the author and the subject, there were we, the future audience, and we were playing our role without knowing it from that very moment. The author was thinking of the relationship between the work and us and was imperceptibly refusing to make it as unexpected, as sharp as possible; he was calculating, he was reckoning upon our reaction, and his action, that is to say his music, was forgetting little by little to be thoroughly itself in order to become that which we were not expecting; he guessed all the points on which we were preparing to greet him and he strove to circumvent us. It is a great temptation for any intelligent artist to have a little fun with those by whom he knows he is being followed and watched. Stravinsky was unable to resist it. *The Nightingale* is not strictly speaking a work; it is after the fashion of cubist canvases, a little esthetic code, exceedingly clever and even profound in spots, full of capital and imperceptible declarations and of professions of faith of unperturbed precision doubtless aimed at making us think, but first at disconcerting us.

Let us refuse to be disconcerted, and since there is a lecture, let us manage to understand it well. The principle which Stravinsky means to insinuate is the very same as that which Cubists and Futurists proclaim with a common accord: it is necessary to give up flattering sensitivity, new art must be intellectualist and address itself only to the faculty of representation within us. Music must therefore cease being emotional. And why should it be only a perpetual invitation to the overflowing of the heart? This is bad manners: it comes too close to us to speak to us, it is too easily familiar with us, it appeals to our sentiments too often, it insists too much on carrying us away, on leading us into consecrated aberrations. Beethoven is the god of passion, that is understood. But he is among all a model not to be followed. Let us leave him to his great soul. Why should one imagine that music should necessarily have, as with him, a moral character? Why should it not be at least for a time as inert and as rough as the voices of nature? It is not a question on making it descriptive or picturesque, but simply mineral, instead of human.

Rousing emotion must be avoided: such is the principle. Here are its consequences:

First, the musician will have to renounce the repetition of themes. Indeed, repetition is a means of rousing sensitivity. When a melody recurs for the second time, it finds in us deeper paths which have been prepared for it in its absence; it becomes more intimate, more ineluctable; since habit weakens our resistance, it (the melody) flows right away to the lowest part of our souls, in the region where we are nothing but confusion and vibration. In order to avoid these indiscreet assaults, each object as far as possible will therefore no longer be named but once; there will be no reappearance of themes. More than anything, the musician will forbid himself to take advantage of time and of the effects which it nurtures; he will proscribe these suspensions and these returns, these cessations and these recalls, these appeasements and these cries which are the very movements of the emotional.

Furthermore, each object will be stated apart from all the others and be surrounded by a blank. It is not a question of touching but of signifying. It is a word that the musician tells us, and he suppresses the sentence which would make it enter into us, which would carry it all the way to our soul. He simply shows; he takes each of his ideas one by one and presents them for an instant: as soon as we have had the material, or rather the legal time to understand it, he withdraws it; he gives only what is needed of it for the mind to be able to track down what he means; right away he cuts the current so that it should go no further than the mind and set our faculties of emotion dancing. This is where the abridged character of his music comes from; resembling in this manner cubist and futurist canvases, it has the appearance of a batch of samples. It is necessary to examine what it contains and turn the page once viewed. We cannot expect to carry it away with us. It is motionless and refuses to carry us. It completely lacks slope, speed, impulse.

Nothing is set so as to permit passage. Between two different objects, even if they are next to one another, why, asks Stravinsky, would one want to create a false auditor, spare his emotion, keep some of it for later, utilize the overflow of his soul, in a word to keep him in an emotional state in which I had first placed him. But my purpose is quite contrary. I shall threfore leave each thing where it is; I shall make it appear in its turn and in its place, without entering it into any ensemble, without tying it either to what precedes or to what follows. I shall proceed item by item.

And indeed all the music of *The Nightingale* makes one think of those lanterns in the second act, so carefully placed on the ground, one beside the other, at quite equal intervals and quite exactly isolated: the music has something about it that is "put there," "on the spot," "no farther than that." Nowhere does it spread; in all its points it seems held back in its enclosure. In it economy is carried to the point of being insulting. Nothing is both more admirable and more exasperating than this perpetual minimum. Basically, it is the song of a nightingale which is being choked. As soon as its voice is about to soar, the musician gives a little twist to its neck: thus its thrills are uttered in a state of fright by which it is impossible that its tormentor secretly not be considerably amused. As a matter of fact, it seems to me that the reasons for which Stravinsky has again picked up the subject of *The Nightingale* are exactly the contrary of those which had made him choose it in the first place. If we go by the first act, which represents the original conception of the work, formerly he had been beguiled by the invitations to expansiveness and the melodic arabesques promised him by the nightingale as a character. But when he comes back to his subject, it is in order to refuse these invitations, to prove to himself, and especially to prove to others, that it is necessary to refuse them. He thinks the demonstration will be all the more striking in that the title of the work makes one expect more improvising, flight, and caprice.[3] Let us hold our nightingale on a leash, let us prevent it from escaping toward space and toward the emotional, and we shall thus mark with decisive evidence the advent of the new art which must be dry, neat, narrow, and mechanical.

Such is the lesson of *The Nightingale*. And I confess first that it delights me; the principles set forth here are particularly appealing to me; even as a good trick played on those who are hostile to them, Stravinsky's work amuses me infinitely. Nothing is funnier than the monstrous brevity of the last act! When the curtain closes slowly, at least ten minutes sooner than expected, one sees the spectators become dumbfounded and all the more comically because they dare not admit it to themselves. As a theoretician, I feel delighted by this malice and I cannot help thinking: "That will teach them!" But finally it is quite a short-lived joy, and it does not compensate for the one which a true work would have given me. Similarly, I fear that the pleasure which Stravinsky savors at the sight of his listeners' disappointment cannot replace the satisfaction which he would have felt if he had created something. I have no criticism of the revolution which he claims to bring about; but I reproach him for having brought it about negatively, whereas he could have done it positively. Instead of wanting to indicate the new values by the negation of the old ones, why did he not propose them directly?

Instead of wanting to deprive music of its emotional character, why did he not simply write music which is not emotional? It is quite natural that a poor cubist, who has only the idea of what should be done and who cannot draw anything from himself to serve as material for his innovations, should persist in trying to mutilate the idea which the past furnishes to him and should think that he is inventing by dint of suppressions. But Stravinsky has extraordinary resources at his disposal. He is in contemporary music the creator *par excellence*. Under the application of his mind alone, the impossible awakens to existence; where he thinks, right away a confused knot forms, like the embryo of a world, which will soon be a new musical being. Even in *The Nightingale*, one sees from time to time emerging from the orchestra sonorous monsters which are whole, alive, armed with all their limbs and of unsuspected origins. Why then did the musician not depend on his inventiveness as he already had in the *Sacre*, for the task of changing values? Precisely, what he invents by himself is something absolutely deprived of expressiveness, of vibration, of tremolo, it is admirable mechanical music; it gives out a sound which is rough, material, and limited. Ah! he does not have to fear that he will let himself go and become emotional. At the present time his inspiration is as naturally inhuman as Mussorgsky was naturally human. Let him give in to his formidable creative power without scheming! And we shall hear rising from the shadow a strange physical tumult which will result in a far more beautiful demonstration than all the little prescriptions of *The Nightingale*.

When Stravinsky again consents to make use of his genius, at the same time, whether he wants it or not, he will again become moving. For when he strives to prevent himself from touching his audience, it is because he fails to make a capital distinction. He is right in not trying to move, but he is wrong in setting out to rebuff [our sensibility] by all manner of means. Indeed, there is an emotion which an artist, even if he does not want to awaken the great human passions which are dormant in our heart, cannot renounce inspiring, lest he, so to speak, deny himself. Every positive creation unleashes in our soul a certain emotion which is immediate, blind, almost automatic. It is a shock which is quite pure and without any qualitative relationship to the content of the work; it is admiration in the etymological sense of the word; it is the abrupt and novel feeling which grips us when we find ourselves before anything that has been wrung from nothingness; it is part of the amazement which the first man must have felt when for the first time he contemplated the work of the Creator. Astonishment, gratitude, and joy enter into it. Today Stravinsky, more than anyone, is appointed to make us feel this emotion; he has no right to disappoint us in this. But I know that he will not disappoint us in it. And if *The Nightingale* has not given me all the contentment which I expected from it, at least it has not lessened my confidence; it is from Stravinsky after all that, given the present state of music, we can hope most reasonably for the most beautiful surprises.

*

From the choreographic point of view proper, the Russian Season this year has been of only mediocre interest. Nijinski's absence has proved to have still graver consequences than I expected: it has left an enormous void. We must say quite loudly: the Russian ballet is Nijinski; he alone animated the whole troupe; he was its inspirer in the proper sense, even when he limited his role to that of performer; now that he has retired, everything collapses; without him Karsavina is but a pleasant dancer; she does not recapture alone that spirit, that accent, that pathetic quality which we have known her to have. Nijinski was more than the inspirer of this troupe; he was its conscience. It was he who forced the others not to be half contented, he who prevented them from taking advantage of their success, from falling back into the open ways, from throwing themselves into the arms of the public. It is he who forced them into research and if I dare say so, into blunder: already last year, the struggle was evident between the tendency of certain members of the troupe—which ones? I do not know—(between those who wanted) to "do Russian ballet" and Nijinski's firm intention "to do it no more." The brake removed, with Fokine's return, the endeavor has tipped entirely in the direction of the easiest course.

Formerly I praised Fokine highly; I even spoke of his genius. Alas! I was wrong. As a dancer he is agile and adroit; but he completely lacks expression. He submitted himself this year to a dreadful trial from which he did not come out to his best advantage: he played *Petrushka*. Ah! how the prison scene, where Nijinski used to put such a profound sense of the tragic, becomes pale and vacuous with Fokine! His interpretation of Stravinsky's masterpiece is as if one removed the lyrics from a melody: the air is still there, but it no longer says anything.

Fokine's importance as an inventor of dances appears today considerably diminished to me. At bottom, he does not know how to cause dance to be born from music; in his ballets they promenade to music, they walk on it, they almost trample it haphazardly; they do not receive it from below, it does not pass into the body, it does not lead it, nor inspire it. For Fokine it is a pretext rather than a law. He listens to it, it gives him the pitch; and in his head he invents with already discovered elements a tableau of movements which will correspond to it, which will produce a symmetrical impression. He translates it in general, in one time, and tries to be faithful to it only from the outside, and only by retaining the same color in his choreography. In reality Fokine is above all a very able stage director. He is much better at dazzling than at moving. What he excels in is composing a show.

That is why his least contestable success this year has been *The Golden Cockerel*[4], which was neither an opera nor a ballet but a show. Although the interpretation he gave of it could have been considered in certain respects as a travesty of the work, I confess I derived extreme pleasure from it. And as a matter of fact, did Rimsky-Korsakov's music not give every license? Easy and happy (it is really astonishing that this be a work of old age), within an ace of banality, but preserved from falling into it by an indescribably charming ingenuity, it is good humored music which, less supercilious than the heirs of the masters, merely smiled at the liberties which were taken with it. Doubtless Fokine's decision to distribute each role in duplicate, both to a motionless singer and to a dancer full of gestures, was at bottom somewhat heavy and ambitious. And indeed the placing of singers dressed in sumptuous clothes and massed on lateral platforms which formed as it were two solemn margins around the animated text gave perhaps a little too monumental an aspect to this fragile work. But how witty, naïve, and joyful was the central staging! And with what intelligence Mlle. Nathalie Gontcharova's décors underscored the wondering and childish character of the music!

Alas! it is doubtless to the platitude, the dull and pretentious vulgarity of Richard Strauss' music that one must attribute the boredom which emanated from *The Legend of Joseph*.[5] Fokine, without a doubt, was also responsible, for he deployed here without restraint this determination to attain art at all costs, this search for magnificent effects which appeared in *The Golden Cockerel* without succeeding in spoiling it. But his bad leanings did not meet any obstacle this time. Quite the contrary, everything encouraged them. We have recognized his gift of feeling truly and of translation with exactness the color of the music entrusted to him. If in *The Legend of Joseph* his staging and choreography were of such an ugly color, the original fault is indeed Strauss'. It is in him that the bad taste with which the work was dripping took its source and prevented us from appreciating as we should have M. Sert's décor and from properly distinguishing the lofty intentions which Count von Kessler had put into his libretto.

Two other spectacles completed the series of "creations.":

Papillons[6] was but a dismal parody of the *Carnaval*.

I did not see *Midas*[7].

NOTES

1   J. Rivière: "La Saison russe," *N.R.F., XII* (July 1914) 150-162.

2   *The Nightingale: Le Rossignol.* Opera by Igor Stravinsky after the fairy tale by Hans Christian Andersen [*Nattergalen*], presented by Diaghilev with sets by Alexandre Benois, at the Paris Opéra, May 26, 1914.

3   It is curious to notice that for the second time with *The Nightingale* Stravinsky undertakes to treat the opposite of a subject. But for the Spring [*Le Sacre du Printemps*] this opposite existed and was something positive which was enough to notice. Here it does not exist, or exists only by a completely arbitrary decree of the author. A nightingale which is afraid of scratching its throat: this may be found in nature, but is not in itself a subject; and the musician may have thought of it only in order to express by this means the principles which he values. [J.R.]

4   *The Golden Cockerel: "Le Coq d'Or."* Opera in three acts by Nicholas Rimsky-Korsakov. Mise-en-scène and choreography by Michel Fokine. Décor and costumes by Nathalie Gontcharova. First performance: Théâtre National de l'Opéra, Paris, May 21, 1914.

"Despite the ballet's triumphant success in Paris and London, Rimsky-Korsakov's widow disapproved of the choreographed version of the opera and forbade Diaghilev to present it again." Boris Kochno: *Diaghilev and the Ballets Russes,* New York: Harper and Row. 1970, 99.

5   *The Legend of Joseph*: "Ballet in one act." Libretto by Count Harry Kessler and Hugo von Hoffmannsthal. Music by Richard Strauss. Choreography by Michel Fokine. Décor by José-Maria Sert. Costumes by Léon Bakst. First performance: Théâtre National de l'Opéra, Paris, May 17, 1914.

"Diaghilev had intended to entrust both the leading role and the choreography to Nijinski, but after their break as a result of Nijinski's sudden marriage and his leaving the company, Diaghilev asked Fokine to create the new ballet....Despite the importance of the Strauss score (the composer conducted at the première) and the sumptuous mise-en-scène by Sert and Bakst, which was inspired by Venetian painting of the Renaissance, particularly the work of Tintoretto and Veronese, *La Légende de Joseph* was not the theatrical event that Diaghilev had expected....Diaghilev had not liked Bakst's sketch for Massine's costume, and he ordered a new sketch from Benois. This costume was a simple goatskin tunic, which led Parisians to dub the ballet 'Les Jambes de Joseph.' " B. Kochno, *Diaghilev,* 95-96.

6 *Les Papillons:* "Ballet in one act by Michel Fokine. (Sequel to *Le Carnaval*). Music by Robert Schumann, orchestrated by Nicholas Tcherepnin. Choreography by Michel Fokine. Décor by Mstislav Doboujinsky. Costumes by Léon Bakst. First performance: Casino, Monte Carlo, April 16, 1914." B. Kochno, *Diaghilev,* 92.

7 *Midas:* "Mythological comedy in one act by Léon Bakst after Ovid's *Metamorphoses*. Music by Maximilian Steinberg. Choreography by Michel Fokine. Décor and costumes by Mstislav Doboujinsky. First performance: Théâtre National de l'Opéra, Paris, June 2, 1914." B. Kochno, *Diaghilev*, 99.

Jacques Rivière prisoner, 1915. (*Photo Rivière*).

quand S. lui a dit que
j'étais « a friend of the 19
Russians ».

5. Avril (Lundi de Pâques)

Pour essayer de me repêcher
du fond de cet abîme où je
suis aujourd'hui, où je tombe
de plus en plus souvent, dont
je ne suis presque pas sorti de
toute cette semaine. Cela me
fait seur, cette décadence main-
   tenant incontestable, cette lente
   victoire de ma situation sur
   ma volonté. Je ne veux pas
mourir ici, je ne mourrai pas ici.
Et c'est pourquoi j'écris ceci comme un remède, moins pour ce
que je vais noter que pour le
secours que ce me sera de le
noter.

Donc ce matin j'ai commu-
nié. Avant-hier cette confession
à la bar. 26, devant tout le
monde, ~~appelé~~ avec ce
cercle dans le dos de ceux qui
attendaient. On devrait pouvoir

A page from Jacques Rivière's *Carnets*.

The Camp's Library. *Left*: Jacques Rivière. *Centre*: The Russian
Interpreter. (1915). *(Photo Rivière)*.

The Camp in Koenigsbrück. (*Photo Rivière*).

I. Jacques Rivière's Study of the Russians During
His Captivity (1914 - 1917)

One month after his pre-war article on Russian music had appeared, Rivière reported for active duty in the French army. Less than three weeks after the outbreak of the war, and after just one day of combat on August 24, 1914, he was captured and removed from the *mêlée* which he was then to observe for three years from a German prisoner-of-war camp, then for the last year of the war, from neutral Switzerland and finally from France.

Following their strong anti-Slavic bias, the Germans delighted in placing French and Russian prisoners in the same camps during World War I, so that the French could see how primitive and unworthy their Russian allies were. At first, this situation had exactly the opposite effect on Rivière. In fact, he became known in his camp for his warm friendliness toward Russian prisoners. The explanation of this reaction can be found both in Rivière's pre-war attitude towards Russian culture and in the detailed record of his impressions while he was a prisoner,

Being in a camp with Russian prisoners was in fact a consolation to him, as his friend Copeau wrote. From the very beginning, Rivière felt so himself, as his notebooks attest.[1] The most important subject of his *Carnets* is his religious crisis. Indeed, these notebooks were to serve as a basis for an apologia of Christianity, which Rivière had decided to write as a token of his gratitude for having been spared. In the face of mortal danger at the front, he had beseeched God for his protection. Under the new circumstances of his existence, he found the religious faith of the Russians inspiring and helpful in surmounting his religious crisis.

Furthermore, after having tried to imagine what the Russians were like for almost a decade on the basis of their music and literature, he at last had the opportunity to live close to them and observe them directly. True, he could not see Russian society as a whole or even a representative segment of it functioning in normal circumstances, but merely Russian men as prisoners of war. Nevertheless, in time he was able to observe many individual types in a fairly broad spectrum of activities among the numerous Russians with wom he personally came into contact in the camp. Fortunately, during the three years which Rivière spent with the Russians, he kept a voluminous diary. In it remarks about the Russians are quite numerous and indicative of his continued interest in them. These notations which amount to approximately forty printed pages also reflect a sincere and profound sympathy for his

Russian comrades. Furthermore, the fact that many of the notations begin with such words as: "I must remember..." indicates that he intended to use his notes to write on the Russians as he did on the Germans and on the French.[2]

As it was masterfully depicted in Alain Renoir's *Grande Illusion*, of which Rivière's descriptions are frequently reminiscent, Russian prisoners lived in much worse conditions than the French, for their country had not signed certain international conventions regarding the treatment of prisoners of war. Furthermore, the Germans' deeply set anti-Slavic bias aggravated the mistreatment of the Russians. The great distances by which they were separated from their country, the war on Russian territory, and the political turmoil it was causing also prevented Russian prisoners from obtaining the help and care French prisoners generally received from home. Packages sent by family and friends enabled Rivière to give most of his camp food ration to his Russian comrades. Naturally, this helped him establish a very friendly rapport with Russian prisoners.

Rivière realized that to understand a people, it is essential to learn their language. He soon came to the realization that "it will be impossible to learn anything about the Russians as long as it will be necessary to go through their interpreters" (*Carnets*, 167). His desire to understand the Russians soon made him undertake the study of their language in which he progressed quite rapidly, for several months later he wrote his wife that he was reading Tolstoy in the original.

Since he also knew German well, he served as camp interpreter. He observed the Germans with acuity but never with sympathy. In this case, his motivation was that of a patriotic Frenchman of his generation, and his study of the Germans' psychology was later to reflect such an attitude.

As for the Russians, Rivière recalled that he had explained his attitude as follows in a conversation he had with several of them:

> I assured them at once of my great sympathy for the Russian people. I told them that before the war I had had a feeling of what they were like; that I dealt with literature; that I had read their authors in French and that all I had learned about their people made me love them in advance, but that since I have come to know them, I love them even more.(Carnets 167)

Rivière also reported with evident pride that he was regarded by all, by some with sarcasm, as the Russians' friend.[3] One should not infer from this, however, that Rivière was unobjective when it came to observing and understanding the Russians. He was quite capable in this as in other situations of keeping feelings apart from thought. In fact, even before his disillusionment with Russia, he made a substantial number of critical remarks on the Russians' psychology and mores.

His wartime remarks about the Russians and their culture tend to fall into several categories: positive and negative aspects of their character; their culture and its effects on them as well as on him; the Russian language; their music and literature—above all Dostoevsky; finally, socialism and the Russian Revolution. Generally, he found the Russians to be wholesome and attractive. Even after he had noticed some of their negative aspects and had experienced some minor disappointments with them, Rivière despised an Englishman for laughing boorishly upon learning of his friendly rapport with the Russians. He found his laughter "gross."

He admired the Russians' lack of aggressiveness and their "attachment to all that they have and at the same time their lack of desire to impose or to claim it against others. They are immensely pleased," he noted "when we go to [their chorus recitals]. But they would not do anything to invite us" (*Carnets, 253*). Curiously he inferred that they were not inclined to be imperialistic and that their empire had grown as a consequence of the vacuums around their country which they had to fill. They too had merely been following their manifest destiny. This, however, corresponded to his impression that the Russians lacked pride--at least a motivating pride. He liked their simplicity with regard to such activities as singing in which they excel. Given the quasi-mystical state in which he lived, Rivière also marvelled at the Russians' naturalness toward religion, the way it was still so much a part and parcel of their everyday life. He was impressed by the religious gestures which they made during the course of the day and by the devotion with which they said their evening prayers. Their prayer recitations in unison and their chants reminded him of *Boris Godunov* (*Carnets, 122*). He was also surprised and touched at their expansiveness and overwhelming tenderness. He liked their sentimentality.

Rivière also liked some Russian traits which are not necessarily positive and which can be grouped under the rubric "primitivism": their violence, especially as he learned about it in their history (*Carnets, 159*), and their "delightful ignorance" (*Carnets, 165*)--in fact, he felt that "the Russian does not stand to gain anything by being cultured" because culture causes him to be presumptuous (*Carnets, 126*). He liked them "less formed" with a "plain and good soul" (*Carnets, 423*). He also admired their extraordinary ability to improvise, as before the war he had been overwhelmed by their extraordinary aptitude for singing and dancing.

102

But as he had to admit to himself, the Russians were not perfect: "How hard it is for me to part with them on so many points! But what can one do against truth?" (*Carnets, 200*). What were these negative points in the Russians' character and their behavior? Rivière could not respect what he regarded as their individual weakness, their resignation to their lot, their lack of glory and military valor, their lack of pride and dignity. In effect he reproached them for lacking the qualities which are seldom found among men who suffer from hunger and harsh treatment and who receive only demoralizing news from home.

These, however, were not his most serious disappointments. Being an individualist first and foremost, one for whom individualism was the beginning of everything, and having "an incurable horror" of totalitarianism (*Carnets, 366*), he was irked by what he called the Russians' "deep sociability," that is to say their "ignorance and incomprehension of what individual life is" (*Carnets, 183*), their propensity for collectivism. He even tried to find a corroboration of his characterization of the Russians in what appeared to him as a "lack of determination" in their language. Consonants and vowels appeared insufficiently differentiated. This naive over-simplification was probably made in a moment of exasperation, for he did like the Russian language. He studied it so diligently on his own initiative for three years that he learned to converse in it fluently and was able to read Russian authors in the original with relative ease.[4] He also admired its stylistic potential. Once he began to despise an English prisoner for his having ridiculed Russian, calling it "a silly language."

A rather meticulous man, as well as an acute and critical observer, Rivière also noted with disappointment the Russians' lack of organization, their disorder, and their unkemptness (*Carnets, 423*). Most of the time, however, these negative reactions appear to have occurred in moments of exasperation and discouragement. Although he did not always esteem them, he continued to like the Russians very much.

As before the war, when he analyzed their music, now, while observing the Russians, he tried to imagine their country and made some deductions about it. As music, literature, and especially Dostoevsky had guided him in his attempt at understanding the people, now the people became for him a clue to the nation as a whole. He felt that like its people, it was not yet completely formed and recalled that even Russia's most forceful rulers could not exact from their subordinates a performance equal to their ambitions. The people could be brutalized, but, remained admirably and despairingly resigned and passive (*Carnets, 195*). He theorized that the cultural lag of the Russians and their passivity were probably due to an insufficiently large intelligentsia, which to make matters worse lived apart from the people. The realization of

these facts and the knowledge he had of abuses by the Russian Orthodox Church prepared him to understand the advent of drastic changes.

All along he learned from Russian prisoners of war and through the
press[5] of the great issues dividing the Russian people and of the progress made by the socialist movement. Although Rivière "hated oppressive doctrines" and abhorred any political philosophy or system which
precludes individualism, when the Russian Revolution did break out,
he thought he understood its causes and even expressed his "solidarity"
with the Russians. At first, he saw the Revolution as a way to improve
the lot of the Russian people rapidly and to help make their civilization
advance. Soon, however, he began to fear the potential threat that the
Revolution would eventually present to the West—that is to say to Britain and France, the cradles of liberalism and the only major countries
with traditions and systems favorable to the full development of the
individual. He did not believe for a moment that Marxism as such could
endure very long, but in one of his extraordinarily visionary flashes he
saw the new system as a step in Russia's evolution. He felt that socialism
might bring Russia to the threshold of greatness. Consequently, his
attitude became ambivalent, for he feared that the rise of Russia would
bring about the decline of Western democracies. Since, and because of
the war, his nationalism had weakened considerably (*Carnets, 422-23*).
He was therefore able to envisage for a moment a new European order
and even a unification of Europe around Russia.

> Never have we been closer to [forming] the United States
> of Europe. The sun rises in the East. And isn't it naturally in
> Russia that it had to appear first, within the people which is
> the least formed, the least conscious of the present, and con-
> sequently the least stubbornly opposed to others—the least
> conscious of individual exigencies, and thereby the least set
> on imposing them on others. (*Carnets, 422-23*)

Many speculated then on the formation of a United States of Europe.
But at that time Rivière was a rare exception to see it from such a perspective and based on so idealized a notion of the Russian character.
What practically all writers had considered as despicable cultural backwardness, he believed to be an asset in the construction of a better
world.

He did not continue very long, however, to place so much hope in the
Russian people. Soon he began to doubt his earlier deductions and
wrote in discouragement: "Maybe it is nothing at all, nothing more than
a new form of Russian disorder, of this weakness of the will, of this lack

of guts which characterizes the Russians" (*Carnets, 423*). Yet in the same breath he returned to his speculation on the possibility that their very defects could actually be compatible with new values. He went so far as to visualize the ultimate: an era of Russian hegemony. Such clairvoyant and visionary speculation alternated in Rivière's mind with notions inspired by his deep religious feelings, his bourgeois prejudices, and especially his nationalism.

He could not overcome his aloofness toward working people, nor was he convinced that real progress could be achieved through social and political reforms. His principal objection to socialism was of a spiritual nature. He refused to be separated from his "dear brothers in thought, from Baudelaire, from Dostoevsky, from all the Christian thinkers" (*Carnets, 424*). Together with them he rejected the very idea of progress. What he especially disliked about socialism was its materialism. Basically, he felt that liberal society was already well organized, and he reminded himself that he should write about that which would be irreparably lost, "if the world such as it is were to be changed, if a socialist regime for example were established." The next day he remarked that he would resent losing at least one thing: "le monde," that is to say a refined elite owing its existence to wealth,[6] the high society Proust was painting (*Carnets, 426-27*).

During the spring of 1917 the rapidly increasing tempo of events in Russia caused him to concentrate his analytical powers even more on the Russians and on the war. The Russian Revolution arising from the war led him to a prolonged reflection on socialism and internationalism. Before the war, to him as to most intellectuals, these two movements had appeared essentially in a theoretical form. The establishment of socialism in Russia—that is to say in a country with enormous potential—impressed upon him both its positive and negative virtualities. Through socialism, he also had a vision of a possible Russian hegemony and its corollary—the decline of the world he loved, liberal Europe. Thus the faith in his coutry was "always exposed to the eclipses of his clairvoyance." He sensed that an inevitable split would divide Europe, and this prospect hurt him deeply. Although nothing could alter his feelings towards the Russians and although his friendship for them made him approve their attempt at establishing socialism, he realized that in the immediate future this would prevent them from assuming their share of the war effort and thereby jeopardize French interests—his interests. He was to remain the prey of this and other dilemmas to the very end of his captivity.

It was under the impact of the Russian Revolution and thanks to a deeper comprehension of Dostoevsky's prophetic interpretation of the

Commune that Rivière came to realize the necessity for Europe to unite. As Dostoevsky had explained it in *The Adolescent* in 1875, Rivière saw a united Europe as the only solution to the new political equation. However, he found it difficult to reconcile the possible new order with his patriotism. He saw his contradictory loves: for his wife and —though chastely—for the wife of his best friend, as correlative to his contradictory political ideals. Recognizing Dostoevsky's influence on his political thought and on his interpretation of current events, he wondered: "Is D[ostoevsky] quite sure that it is only as a Russian that he feels so European? Is it not because Russia is all dripping with Christianity?" (*Carnets, 448*). It was Christianity that made Rivière so receptive to the Russians, especially to Dostoevsky, and perhaps even made him accept briefly the concept of socialism.

However, in May 1917, shortly before he was to leave Germany for internment in Switzerland because of impaired health, he momentarily came to despise the Russians for being on the verge of abandoning their allies by withdrawing from the war. This hurt him deeply, but he remained convinced of Russia's mysterious mission and his feelings were not changed for long by these events.

> I see now a new, a deeper meaning which I could not have foreseen for my love of Russia, so mysterious, from the beginning. I understand all the ideas that she [Russia] carries, the seed which is in her must have really been placed in me, at the beginning, at my birth itself. By what wind had [the seed] been carried? (*Carnets, 448*)

The time when he was writing this also corresponded to his greatest admiration for Dostoevsky, not as the master of the novel but as the thinker, the visionary who had foreseen the need for a Europe united around Russia, and Dostoevsky the humanitarian who spoke of the mystic bond uniting all men. During most of the captivity—especially the first year—Rivière had read religious authors both for spiritual inspiration and because he was gathering ideas and facts for the apologia of Christianity he planned to write. As early as February 4, 1915, he recalled that Dostoevsky had also spent four years in a penitentiary. His fortitude was a source of inspiration for Rivière. For the following two years, he progressively added to his secular readings, primarily French classics. However, during the spring of 1917 he was reminded by events of Dostoevsky's extraordinary speculations on the fate of Europe, which he reread in *The Adolescent*. At first he remarked that he had been closer to Dostoevsky in the past and reiterated some reservations about his art. Soon, however, he fell under Dostoevsky's spell again and began to write about him with reverence. He found some consolation at this time in the analogies between Dostoevsky's and his own life and in the privilege of being a member of the quasi-mystical body formed by those who admired Dostoevsky.[7] Once he had reestablished contact with Dostoevsky's thought, Rivière wrote his long informal essay on all the important issues of the time—patriotism, internationalism, liberalism, socialism. There is no doubt that on the eve of his being released no author influenced his thought as much as the Russian novelist.

In the sping of 1917 Rivière was considerably weakened for having spent three years in captivity. For months he had been living in the hope of being selected for internment in Switzerland. The moment of deliverance came for him at last. On June 14, 1917 he finally arrived in Zurich. Several days later he wrote to his wife:

> Never have I been as sad as these last few days. It is as if my body were out of prison, but my soul has not yet been returned to me. And I am not sure of ever recovering it...
> I am still at the bottom of a deep night, and very badly awakened. Help me. (*Carnets, 453-54*)

He was reunited with his wife and daughter only in July 1917. Then began his long recovery. Soon he resumed a very active life as a writer and lecturer. Out of patriotic duty, and also to free himself from his memories of captivity, he first wrote *L'Allemand*, a controversial book on the German personality. At the same time, as one might expect, he anxiously continued to follow the evolution of the war and to take a deep interest in the course of events in Russia. In fact, the numerous articles on the Russian Revolution that he gathered at that time indicated that he probably envisaged writing on the subject. None of the writings anterior to 1919 are helpful, however, in following the evolution of his thought on Russia.

Shortly after arriving in Switzerland, he began to ask his friends to help obtain his repatriation. Weak as he was, he wished most of all a front-line assignment, probably in the hope of wiping off three years of humiliation and perhaps also to avenge Alain-Fournier who had been lost in the first months of the war. When he learned this was forbidden under the agreement which had made his liberation possible, he asked for a desk job in Paris so as to be able to resume writing. During the long months of waiting, his friend Jean Schlumberger, who occupied an influential post in Intelligence, offered to obtain for him a responsible assignment as diplomatic attaché to the French ambassador in Switzerland. He only showed some interest in this possibility when it became apparent that his other option was pacification duty in Morocco. On the other hand, he was most willing to accept an assignment anywhere in Russia. For the opportunity to know this country at first hand and witness the momentous events occurring there, he was ready to be separated again from his wife and child—a separation from which he had suffered intensely for three years.

Given Rivière's strong interest in Russian music and literature, which had already resulted in a number of important essays, and given the opportunity he had to observe Russians, one is surprised that he did not write a substantial essay as he soon did on the Germans and as he had clearly intended to do on the Russians. True, there was no patriotic urgency to do so as he felt there was for *L'Allemand*, which he regarded as a token contribution to the war effort. More importantly, having had regrets about certain aspects of his work on the Germans, he probably feared he could not maintain sufficient objectivity--or competency--in his intended work on the Russians. The two important essays "*Décadence de la liberté*" (1919) and "*De Dostoevski et de l'insondable*" (1922) on the subject express or betray a disenchantment with all things Russian, due however, far more to the course of events in Russia amplified by the accounts of numerous emigrés[8] who were arriving in France than to a fundamental and an irrevocable change of attitude toward the Russian people.

NOTES

1   Jacques Rivière, *Carnets 1914-1917,* Paris: Fayard, 1974), p.191.

2   *L'Allemand, souvenirs et réflexions d'un prisonnier de guerre* (Paris: Gallimard, 1918; Réimpression augmentée d'un avant-propos, 1924); *Le Français* (Paris: Claude Aveline, 1928).

3   *Ibid.* pp. 155, 178 and elsewhere. In his analysis of Pierre Pascal's comments on the Russians made by French military advisors in St. Petersburg during World War I, Ioannis Sinanglou shows that most Frenchmen misunderstood Russian attitudes and intentions. Sympathetic observers like Rivière and Pascal came closest to the truth in their analysis and interpretations.

4   Rivière's notebooks contain a considerable number of passages in Russian, including long quotations.

5   Rivière surveyed the press and prepared daily reports and weekly analyses for his comrades in the camps.

6   Rivière was not personally wealthy but of bourgeois background.

7   In March 1917, Rivière had read Rozanov's introduction to *Polnoe sobranie Socineij F. M. Dostoevskogo. Tom pervyj, chast' pervaja.* S-Petersburg Izdanie A. F. Marksa: 1894. Rozanov imagines a vast community of readers assembled around Dostoevsky's works (*Carnets, 411-417).*

8   During the twenties, émigré Russian writers such as Vladimir Nabokov, A. Levinson, Vladimir Pozner and Henri Troyat endeavored to correct French views of the Russian people as inspired by Dostoevsky.

108

2. Excerpts from Jacques Rivière's *Carnets 1914 - 1917* with Commentaries

> "All my thought associations were literary."
> J.R., September 1914

Although he kept a diary only from the beginning of the war to the end of his captivity in Germany, Rivière had been in the habit since adolescence of recording his activities in weekly letters to his family, especially his aunts in Bordeaux. It was no doubt the impossibility of communicating freely with his family that made him decide to keep a diary. This diary was finally published in its entirety in 1974 under the title of *Carnets (1914-1917)*. It is subdivided into a *"Carnet de Guerre"* which contains a detailed account of Rivière's brief campaign and of his initial experiences as a prisoner of war. Then follow the fourteen precisely numbered and dated notebooks which contain a description of his activities and, more importantly, summaries of his thoughts and feelings. The principal theme is a mystical quest for God. The substantial excerpts of these "carnets," which were published shortly after his death, bore the title *A la trace de Dieu* (In God's wake), a phrase Rivière himself used in his Carnets.

For the first three and one-half months of his captivity, Rivière seemed to be totally absorbed by his remorse for not having given sufficient spiritual support to his brother-in-law, Henri Alain-Fournier, who, he had since learned, had disappeared in combat and was probably dead. He felt and even greater guilt for having gone to war with an impure heart: while he had remained in love intellectually and spiritually with his wife Isabelle, he had fallen passionately in love with a woman who, to make matters worse, did not fully return his love—not because her lover was perhaps her husband's best friend, but because she was spoiled and superficial. Thus Rivière was a man tormented by guilt and remorse with respect to his now-killed brother-in-law, his wife, and his beloved's husband. That was not all. Although still not completely cured from scepticism, in the thick of battle, seeing comrades falling dead or wounded, spontaneously and with almost visceral faith, he had entrusted his life to God. He remained convinced during the three years he spent in Germany, and perhaps later as well, that God had listened to his prayer and that his survival was miraculous. An honest and logical man, Rivière felt that he had to bring his life in line with his faith. He began by leading a profoundly pious life. In the camp this was relatively easy. But he long continued to be tormented by the enduring love he had for his friend's wife. Another cause for guilt and remorse which he also tried to remedy was the feeling that he had not done his duty as a soldier because he had surrendered after only one day of combat. Once he had regained his strength and bearings, Rivière escaped from his camp and almost managed to reach the Dutch border. His principal reason for having attempted to escape was an imperative desire to return to the front and to do his duty. He almost paid with his life for his desire to make his life conform with his principles. But his attempted escape brought him at least some peace in his spiritual relationship with his country. Later, he was to try to fulfill his duty again, but as a writer. Indeed, no sooner had he been interned in Switzerland than he hastened to write a book on the Germans (*L'Allemand*),[1] which he regarded as his personal contribution to the war effort. The writing of this controversial book seemed to purge him of the passionate patriotism which he had felt as had almost all his contemporaries everywhere. After the war he was among the first to advocate Franco-German cooperation.

While living his intense mystical experience, Rivière also attempted to sort out his sentiments. Perhaps for lack of other means, as a writer he naturally turned to literature and wrote a quasi-autobiographical novel, *Aimée*.[2] This, too, had the effect of diminishing the intensity of his forbidden love and thereby to relieve his emotional tension as well as his feeling of guilt.

During his quest for God which brought about at least a temporary realignment of his life and emotions with his faith and piety, Rivière's first distraction was occasioned by the presence of Russian prisoners of war who were brought to his camp a little over three months after he had arrived there himself. The intensity of his spiritual experience necessarily had decreased somewhat by then and the Russians were to provide him with a welcome distraction and, more importantly, a means of reestablishing contact with his pre-war interests. From the beginning, Rivière realized that the Russians' presence was for him a blessing and an opportunity. He was first touched by their spirituality, and the writer in him immediately felt that destiny had placed him in the presence of rich material he should gather for future literary use. And thus, from the very first day, Rivière began to make notations on the Russians in his notebooks. On the second day he reminded himself in a note that he ought to write down what he had witnessed his Russian neighbors do. Judging by the nature of Rivière's notations which record incidents, behavior, conversations, and the interpretations the Russians inspired in him, he clearly intended to use this material in essays and even perhaps in works of fiction. The opportunity to observe real and live Russians inevitably reminded Rivière of Dostoevsky's novels in which he had admired swarming and teeming life as well as profound spirituality, a dualism which corresponded so well to his experience of the moment. Thus Dostoevsky's presence grows in importance in the notebooks, especially as his conversations with socialistically minded Russian prisoners led him to the burning subjects of fraternity, of Christian charity, of peace in social justice. As the moment of his liberation approached, Rivière had strayed considerably from spirituality to ideological and even political preoccupations, to a considerable extent through the influence of the Russians in general and Dostoevsky in particular. Thus, the Russians' role in Rivière's evolution should hardly be disregarded, as it has largely been so far.

*

Our intention here is to gather and to translate the passages, notations and reflections pertaining essentially to the Russian personality and thought as well as to Dostoevsky. These quotations will sometimes be accompanied by a commentary which may be useful for some readers. Several more purely descriptive passages will be included here as examples of the sketches Rivière recorded clearly for future use in works of fiction he doubtless hoped to write. Finally, the reader must bear in mind that they were not prepared for publication by Rivière himself.

*

Rivière saw Russians for the first time on December 14, 1914, and he recorded the event as follows:

> First contact with the Russians. At once there was something about them which gave them a *reality*...A nature...
> The chorus of the first roomful made me feel a deep emotion upon finding myself all of a sudden in the presence of something like an unpolished, roughly interpreted Mussorgsky, but it was pure and the soul that appeared in it was a part of my own. I realized this well by the way it moved me. They had young and hard faces like brutal and pure children; the little one who sang the solos with that weak, clear and hesitant voice, and the other one sitting on a chair and whom I could only see against the light had a violent and new air. The hooligan, with his back leaning against the column, with his cluttered and scoundrelly voice, and those wild cries he uttered at the beginning of each refrain; the one

who was standing next to him, who seemed to be whispering and who sang as if he were praying. How I loved them! (118)[3]

In spite of the absence of privacy in camp life and the opportunities for offensive behavior, Rivière never ceased to have deep sympathy and affection for his fellow Russian prisoners.

In the following passage, obeying his own resolution made the previous day, Rivière recorded on December 16 his observation of the way his neighbor went to bed:

> He had fallen asleep around eight, his boots on under his large coat thrown over himself like a blanket, his cap over his eyes. At the moment I was about to give in to sleep, I saw him getting up brusquely as if caught in error and looking around; then seeing that the others were sleeping, he carefully set his tent canvas on the straw and began to inflate his rubber pillow by blowing into it as softly as possible. Then he undressed quickly, throwing his jacket, his belt, his suspenders in the trough[4] and lay down under his tent, under his blanket which he had pulled over his head.
>
> His name is: Jacob Fédiouk. (120)[5]

The next day, December 17, Rivière wrote:

> This morning, both awake, each still entangled in his blanket, Fédiouk gave me a good smile by way of a morning greeting. But it is only a long while later, after we had been up and after he had washed, that he came up to me to give me a handshake and say good morning. This little ceremony had a kind of familiar solemnity to make up for its lateness. Already yesterday morning he had given us a handshake only long after we had gathered and suddenly, as if the moment for it had arrived, as the hour to pray arrives. (121)

On December 16:

> To eat, Fédiouk remains seated rather far from the table; but he does not lean over it. He dips into his bowl with his ladle-shaped spoon from a distance and quite delicately makes it travel to his mouth.

*

Their evening prayer: a psalmody in which for a few minutes only was I able to find some indices, some traces of the religious songs of *Boris* [*Godunov*].

*

The little Russian quarter-master-sergeant who is so ceremonious, who bows in front of each of us before shaking our hands, how he was waltzing the other evening, as straight as a pole planted on a turning platform transporting him without moving him, without damaging him. (122)

As frequently became the case at the end of the next day's usual spiritual and highly personal reflections, Rivière recorded an observation on the Russians:

December 19, 1914

Fédiouk hums all day and from time to time he also burps gently.

He has such an exquisite way of smiling and identifying himself to our discovery, uttering Ahs! when Lauriol[6] or I notice a Miapku Chak [sic][7] in a word which he has just told us.

This night, when I was awake, I found he had completely disappeared under his blanket from under which only the valve of his rubber cushion stuck out as if he were a submerged diver whose presence can only be detected by the pipe which enables him to breathe. (124)

December 22:

Conversation in poor German with Nickel,[5] the Russian interpreter. He is more complex than I first thought he was. Is he really a non-commissioned officer as his overcoat claimed it to be the case for the first time [sic]? Or had he taken someone else's? Be that as it may, there is in him a kind of reserve, an aloofness which the delightful humility of his face had first concealed from me. There is also a little vanity: he asked me if I was a marksman so as to have the opportunity to tell me that he was first-rate and that he had won a watch: *eine Uhr*.

At the same time he has a certain tendency to put himself on the side of those who are highest ranking in dignity, a kind of imperceptible way of separating himself from the mass (i.e., his slightly scornful attitude toward Karol[5] whom he doubtless finds too good, easy-going—as well as his way of giving orders to his own men, his change of tone when he addresses them). He has republican views which he barely let me perceive. All these elements compose a personality which is more clever, more pliable, and more varying than I had first perceived it, less *Russian* in the excessively simple sense in which I had understood this word until now. But I may be instead in the process of discovering a personality which is more truly Russian than the one I was imagining in the abstract.

Already as of now I do not believe the Russian improves by educating himself. Certain parts of his soul are too fragile, too unstable. A minute thing may be sufficient to corrupt it, to "make it turn"; it needs to remain absolutely virgin in order not to become villainous. The stem of a Russian's character is too weak for him to grow straight. (125-126)

Naive though they may appear, the above remarks show how keenly interested Rivière was in penetrating the mystery of the Russian soul. This was the reason he undertook the study of the Russian language (167). He shows here an incipient tendency to idealize Russians as being plain, good, pure and primitive—a notion he had gathered especially through his contact with Russian music and which corresponded to stereotypes held by Westerners sympathetic to the Slavs.

December 23, 1914

When the other day Ch[acornac][8] told this Russian in a teasing way: "Russians kaput!" his face filled with consternation as he sat on the corner of his bed. He seemed somewhat like Jacqueline[9] when she grieves about something: there is a slight shade of comedy, but at the same time the imperceptible amusement of a child who is learning to feel. At the same time he seemed to be asking for forgiveness from the bottom of his heart in the name of his entire people from this Frenchman whom quite naturally he regarded as his superior. But first and foremost, submerging everything else,

I could read on his face the disarming resignation, the quickness to accept situations, which is the profound cause of all Russian defeats. There is no cowardice in these people; they do not run before danger. But as soon as they touch an obstacle, they stop. There is a terrible absence of anger, a radical inability to get on top of the obstacle, to overcome it, to "penetrate it." No plan, no intention is held to for an instant in the face of contrary events. That is the drawback of humility: just as the Russian does not extend himself beyond what he is, he does not imagine himself either better or stronger than he is, his designs do not overshadow facts; they limit themselves to facts, stop at them, their designs become at once circumscribed within facts; it does not occur to a Russian that what has sprung up in his mind could be something more than what happens and that it could be more deserving of materializing. He immediately exchanges what he had conceived for what happens. He is incapable, were it for a minute, of preferring one over the other.

*

There was something more in him: a delightful and childish readiness to accept suggested feelings. The *immediate* way in which his face reflected sudden consternation, the weak, timid, and charming "oh!" he uttered--and as soon as we had reassured him, the instantaneous reawakening of his joy, the brightening up of all his traits, with, deep down, the pleasure of being returned to his carefree state, to be permitted again to worry about nothing which to him appeared like a second light. (128-129)

Rivière did not share most Westerners' and even most Frenchmen's scorn for the Russians. In fact, as if wishing to have grounds to admire them more, he was exasperated by the apparent weakness he observed in individual Russians. Although his commentary is not without exaggeration and errors, many would concur with him when he points to a certain inferiority complex. This is perhaps at the root of Russians' hospitality and respectful consideration for foreigners, often exceeding such feeling for their compatriots. Similarly, the extraordinary curiosity and appreciation they show for the outside world and foreign things cannot be explained only by the confinement in which Russians have had to live.

December 28, 1914

Last evening, the Russian show in the sergeants' former barracks. It was nothing at all. Several hung blankets, a curtain pulled with wires, stools on which the boards forming the stage rested, a soberly scratched violin backstage.

But what a knack for improvising! What vivaciousness of imagination! How that took right away! Each actor had created for himself a charming and grotesque silhouette by means of imperceptible changes in his uniform. At once he would stand out and from the first signify something. (139)

December 31, 1914

The other day, Lavrov[5] and the big blond fellow from Smolensk insisted that Nickel was not Russian: "Nickel nixt [sic] russe!" they answered with obstinacy to all our attempts at demonstrating the contrary. And on the map of Russia they would trace an approximate circle which excluded all the Black Sea region, Poland, Finland. They explained to us as best they could that those countries were Russian "colonies" as Morocco is a colony of France. I was quite happy to feel that they were proud to be purely Russian and to see that they considered themselves in a way aristocratic. I can say that until now they have never caused me to be disillusioned even once. (142)

As with most Westerners then and even today, Rivière originally had no idea of the great differences existing among the peoples who made up the Tsarist Empire and the Soviet Union today. Significantly, he had a distinct preference for "pure Russians," doubtless because he saw them as the creators of the music and literature he knew.

Fédiouk has five children. He reenlisted. He works hard on his German all day long and does not make any visible progress. "I like that!" as Lauriol would say.

I must remember the delightfully dismayed tone with which the actors of the other day said, "Kaput!" to me, showing the already hung blankets, the curtain already installed, when I told about the objections the warrant-officer had to their show.

The one who looked like Maritchou. The little tenor who
is a movie producer. The plain and strapping way in which
he planted himself on the edge of the stage to sing, with his
fist on his hip. The one who had a long and plain face lit by a
splendid look and who must be, although I did not recognize
him right away, the comedian with the bass voice whom I
liked so much that evening. In fact, I am certain it is he. The
Nijinski way with which, once the show was over, he pretended to rape the one dressed as a woman.

Korol. He has such a happy, such an eager way of saying:
"ui, ui," when we have understood something. His childish,
desolate, and resigned look when after long explanations he
is forced to say "Ze comprends pas."

I must remember the group which the other evening formed around Fédiouk who spoke to them as they were leaning
on the bin. Sweetness of their voices, intimacy, almost tenderness. (143)

Rivière's repeated resolve to remember certain Russian characters and
scenes formed by them indicates his intention to use these sketches in
future works. Significantly, he again related the human reality existing
before his very eyes to his memory of artistic representation of it. As
usual, he stressed most sympathetically the simplicity he was able to
observe.

January 9, 1915
My vanity is far from dead. The pleasure I feel at the kind
of respect I sense around me here. The pleasure at being sa-
luted by the Russians, among others, by the interpreter of
the fourth barrack who is far from being congenial. (155)

As an interpreter of French and German, who also had a reading knowledge of English and Italian and who was rapidly learning Russian, Rivière enjoyed the respect of all his fellow prisoners. His prestige was en-
hanced by the fact that he prepared and delivered daily news analyses
based on his reading of newspapers written in various languages. Significantly, he was especially pleased to enjoy the respect of the Russians.

January 12, 1915
Why is the Russians' violence so appealing to me? What
kind of joy can I find in it?

How admirable the story of Grand-Duke Nikolaï Niko-
laïevich who on arriving in Warsaw called the governor to
give him a thrashing because the latter had executed his order late!

And the way in which he rushed at the officers and ripped
off their epaulettes!

The tragic situation of a man who tries to do something
for his people and who does not manage to succeed in it. He
is alone with a will in the midst of this multitude. (159)

What Rivière seems to admire in this episode of Russian history is not
Russian violence as such but the violent will with which a Russian leader saw to the execution of a national policy. Implicitly, he draws a severe deduction from the lethargy of the Russian people which appears
incapable of greatness except under terror. One could also add that
being quite authoritarian himself, Rivière may have admired the forceful exercise of authority.

While studying Russian early in 1915, Rivière was also beginning to
reflect on such questions as war, pacifism, the social and political implications of Christianity and especially Catholicism. Under the influence of French and Russian comrades, socialism then appeared as an
important theme in his thought.

January 18, 1915
The other day Nickel said: "You know this great forest
which you see over there, well it goes without interruption
all the way to the Karpathians." And what he said about the
Argonne Forest.

Delightful kind of ignorance. The kind that creates le-
gends. (165)

Once more, Rivière expresses his delight at the form of ignorance he
noticed in a Russian. Not in a patronizing way, but because this corresponded to his concept of what he had imagined the Russians to be like,
i.e., primitive, good, and pure. This attitude betrays in him, a modern
Westerner, an unconscious longing for a mythical primitivism, a paradise lost.

Reflecting with satisfaction on the progress he had realized in becoming humbler, Rivière remarked that he was totally indifferent to
being assimilated to the Russian interpreters—which he regarded as
degrading. He went on extrapolating a moral lesson from Dostoevsky
to whom he referred for the first time. Dostoevsky was to occupy an

118

increasing place in Rivière's thoughts and his evolution during the next two and one-half years during which he remained a prisoner of war.

February 4, 1915

Dostoevsky's concept of atonement, his idea of the fecundity of sin: how profound, how admirable it is! How immense are the regions one discovers as soon as one is past the zone of vanity, as soon as one ceases to consider the effect one can produce on others, as soon as one thinks only about what one has done, what one does, about the value, the importance that our actions can have in themselves.

Today, during fatigue-duty, in the midst of all those Russians pushing tip-trucks in that immense snow-covered moor landscape, I was thinking of Dostoevsky in the house of the dead. May my soul break here, open itself to charity, like his! May I rot in order to germinate! May all the careful little compartments into which I am divided give, crack, be transformed into a perfect mash!

May I learn charity, as perhaps I have learned patience! (178)

In this poignant prayer in which he invokes Dostoevsky's name, Rivière is still quite deeply steeped in his experience.

February 10, 1915

Fatigue-duty at the sand quarry (of Zietsch). The Russians have a strange ability to establish themselves. In the evening, the way they move into our quarters to read the newspaper, and nothing could make them budge. I think of Dostoevsky, of his characters who put down roots and who no longer leave.... It isnot exactly for lack of tact. It is rather due to ignorance and incomprehension of what individual life is. They disturb it without reserve because they do not recognize it, because they do not know what it is.

And it is indeed striking to see here how little they live *against* each other! Whereas the French each have a separate and aggressive development, they do not need to distinguish, to impose themselves one upon the other. They remain together in a kind of semi-realization of a vague and common life, the one which is expressed in their songs and which is so lively and so indeterminate. It is not somnolescence at all, not Asiatic stupor, but a profound "sociabi-

lity." Hence all their charm and all their faults. How delightful they are to approach, the absence of sting in them, which
is so pleasant in comparison with the little French will, with
the little stubbornness about himself which the Frenchman
has. The latter will throw in your face all he's got; he presents himself to be taken or left whole and sees infinite pro-
vocations in everything that you undertake. But the Russians do not hold up: they are so weak, so fused. The way
they beg for tobacco; their habit of selling everything they
have and now even the bread that is given to them at fatigue-
duty. They suffer from a lack of determination (in the passive sense). (182-183)

The first thing that should be remembered about the above paragraph is
that when Rivière projects an almost cruel light into the Russian psyche,
he does not do so because of disillusion and even less to favor the French
by contrast. He is simply seeking the truth although he may be erring,
especially regarding his growing conviction about the weakening or
lack of determination of the Russian personality.

February 20, 1915

The Russians! Above all they lack glory and boldness.

*

For the Russians the border is too far. That is why they
cannot be a militarist nation. They have no pressure to bear.
And they have no spring. When they attack, they have to
take the offensive on the site, assume it all. There is nothing
within them to make them rush forth.

Russia is essentially the country of instituions. All her
virtues consist in ties, in a faithfulness, in a relationship to
that which is, which holds, which subsists. Why fight? They
have nothing to put forth. Everything already exists. And
their great science, the one in which they surpass the rest of
the world in competency, consists in knowing how to refer to
the [institutions]. (190-191)

Although Rivière seems to have vaguely perceived the importance of
what is now referred to as the "aparat," his rash generalizations, which
history has shown to have been so erroneous, were clearly inspired by
the disappointment felt among the French over the performance of the
Russian army in combat.

120

The other day, I was saying to myself as I was going to
bed: "With me happiness is becoming an illness. It is something I have caught here, like lice."

And in Copeau's letter, this sentence: "I understand very
well how you could have organized your life and be happy
there. Blessed be the destiny that brought you in contact
with Russian prisoners." This sentence made me suddenly
understand what "I had."

Yes, this happiness is the same as the one Dostoevsky had
in the penitentiary; it is the happiness found in the pit of any
great humiliation, of all trampling of the being. It is joy
which made Dmitri Karamazov rapturous when he was
about to leave for Siberia. The greatest, the surest, the holi-
est of all! The joy of the person who has nothing to boast
about, of the one in whom bottom has been touched. A
rising tide, a hymn, something too full, infinitely overflowing, almost bombastic and ridiculous. Ceaselessly
maintained, ceaselessly renewed from great internal sources.
That is indeed what I feel, that is indeed what I was carried
away by on the 17th during fatigue-duty. Like the tree cut
open and from which sap bleeds. Like the grain which rots
and which germinates. A live vein in me has been pierced,
and here is this liquid which pours out, my wealth, my food,
the nourishment which I am no longer lacking. (191-192)

Under Dostoevsky's invocation this mystical praise develops into a
prayer in which Rivière asks to be taught charity.

My God, keep this wound open, widen it still more. May I
at last know charity. I do not have the presumption to believe that I might have already reached it. I know well all that
I am lacking in order to attain the immensity of Dostoevsky's soul. (How far I am still from a nominal, a personal
love for each of my companions here! Even if I go a little
further than most of the others, if I do not stop at the first
lines of defense, there still is not this gripping of the guts, this
upsetting caused by charity which Dostoevsky felt.) But
started, oriented by this happiness, it can come. I ask you
for it, my God! So that I may be good for someone before
dying, for something other than directing sentiments and
ideas. (192)

The Russians and specifically Dostoevsky are frequently referred to in
Rivière's prayers. This shows that there was a relationship between his
profound sympathy for them and his religious experience. As we shall
see when Rivière's religious fervor decreased, his objectivity and severity in observing the Russians increased.

> March 6, 1915
> The other day, the way Fédiouk read the punishment in-
> flicted on the Russians who had tried to flee. The infinite
> resignation in his voice when he pronounced the last words:
> *Dresdinié Dpecdu* [sic].[10] An ending quite à la Mussorgsky.
> All that is admirable and despairing about Russia! (195)

Here we have again an example of the way in which Rivière established
a relationship between a real situation and an esthetic experience quite
removed in time.

> March 12, 1915
> The "wet bird drying" aspect of the Russians.
> The lack of determination in their language: all the conso-
> nants half this, half that: semi-vowels. Everything lies in the
> inflection: tenderness, childishness, all the resources ne-
> cessary to express amusement and resignation. (197)

Much later, Rivière was going to return to these curious psychological
extrapolations in his observations on the Russian language.

> March 18, 1915
> The Russians: their distribution of bread in the morning,
> with a little wooden scale, asking: "Kamu?"[11] [sic] The coffee
> they made all day long with roasted bread crumbs. No better
> symbol of their immense childishness.
>
> How hard it is for me to part with them on so many
> points! But what can one do against truth? (200)

Rather than to pretend to be drinking coffee as such, the Russians had
actually improvised a way to make their own drink called *kvas*. This is
not therefore an example of childishness on the part of the Russians.
Instead, Rivière simply did not know about *kvas*.

> April 5, 1915
> The singing of the Russians this morning under the firs...
> The marvelous little choir leader with his fine face, his eagle
> nose, his jacket and his belt, his way of beating time...Incre-
> dible perfection of the choruses. The little bass with his thick
> lips...The one on the left, crossing himself all the time....

122

The Russians are so attached to all that they have, and at the same time they have little desire to impose it on others or to set it up against what others have. They are immensely pleased when we attend [their performances]. But they would do nothing to call you.

Far from wanting to spread and spill beyond their borders, they look to the center of the Empire, toward Moscow and Petersburg. That is the direction of their desire.

Curiously, Rivière is not taking into account Russian imperialism and the expansionism it led to in the East and West, nor did he seem to be aware of the calling to greatness felt by the Russians.

*

Yesterday, there was the Russian who had gathered some wood under the firs and who was called by the sentry. How he tried to explain, his repeated salutes, his evident desire to get away and to keep the wood. He showed in such an expressive way that he was cold. He could hardly imagine that he could do something other than to submit.

April 9, 1915
The day before last, Mitzsenko[5] said of the choir: "Yes, it is good. But they cannot sing as in Russia." They are still attached to their holy places.

"If you could hear this in Moscow and in Petersburg...." Their eyes are always turned in that direction. (208)

April 18, 1915
The Russians' songs, this evening in the open air...Their way of doing this as if it were "only that"...When I think how Bach's divine simplicity is still monumental by comparison with that, I understand the foreigners' bewilderment in the presence of Russian art; they must wonder over what was announced and how it passed them by. "What is that? We do not see anything." (211)

Again basing himself on an excessively small sampling of Russian art performed in less than adequate circumstances, Rivière evidently exaggerated its simplicity and peculiarity.

April 19, 1915
The Russians came without being told to do so, behind the section I commanded only so as to avoid being commanded by one of their own. (212)

After having recorded the expression of disappointment of a Russian prisoner over a package he had received, Rivière seemed pleased to have observed this manifestation of proud behavior in a Russian:

> April 23, 1915
>
> The day before last, as I was offering biscuits to Lavrov and Aphonin[5] because before lunch Aphonin had told me that his head was turning, I had placed the biscuits on the table next to them as if to make them accept. Without saying anything, Lavrov picked up the dictionary and indicating a word with his finger, he handed it to me saying gravely: "We have nothing, but what we have left is.....And I read: "...conscience."
>
> I blushed but indicated to him that I found his scruple ridiculous. As a result he accepted my biscuits. Did he have the firm intention of refusing them?
>
> Aphonin did not seem to fully understand his comrade's demonstration. (215)
>
> April 24, 1915
>
> The other day, the Englishman, always with that naïve and gross laughter, said, of Russian: "It is a silly language."[12] (217)

Clearly, Rivière had nothing but scorn for this simplistic Englishman.

> May 2, 1915
>
> When a Russian who had to leave was asked about his religion he at first did not understand; then the interpreter repeated:
>
> "Russian religion?"
>
> "Russian, thank God!" he answered briskly, with a kind of astonished little laugh which was so happy.
>
> The whole Russian soul is there. They are so happy not to be anything other than what they are!
>
> And when one thinks of the infinite number of horrible faults that this sentiment excludes, one forgives them the few that it implies. (219-220)

Apparently Rivière did not realize that when asked about their religion, Russians ordinarily specified that they were Russian orthodox as opposed to, for example, the Uniates.

Between May and November Rivière went through a period of deep depression. The Russians were moved to another camp in mid-July. He made his escape on the 25th. Recaptured and severely punished, he was only able to resume writing regularly in his diary in October. The failure of his escape plunged him again into a phase of profound mysticism. It is through his reading of Gogol that he resumed his contact with the Russians.

> November 1,1915
>
> Regarding *Dead Souls* (Cantos XI and XII), it will be necessary to characterize "infinity" in Russian thought and to show precisely its nature through examples. Gogol is an admirable example of this union between the sharpest and most active precision and of those great and sudden vistas which are born in the very midst of the tightest remarks. Infinity pouring out (as if obtained from the very pressure of the halt), and standing out in the midst of the most hurried sentences....Use the passage on speed at the end of Song XI and the invocation to Russia at the beginning of the same Song. (271)

Although he had frequently recorded details about Russians with the evident intention of using them in a future work, here Rivière actually states his desire to write a work on Russian mentality.

In the absence of Russian prisoners in his camp, Rivière maintained contact with their culture through extensive reading of Dostoevsky, Gogol, and Tolstoy. He also had lengthy conversations with a Polish Jew, Teitelbaum,[5] about the Russians' hospitality, which made Rivière realize with remorse that the much better supplied French prisoners had used the Russians as servants in exchange for food. They also discussed Tolstoy's reputation in Russia and socialism. Teitelbaum, more than any other individual he encountered, seems to have made him come to grasp with the Jewish question and with socialism.

Until mid-July 1916, Rivière's diary is kept quite sporadically, and only one significant event involving a Russian is evoked and deserves to be communicated here. A Russian prisoner who had escaped and was recaptured naïvely designated Rivière to the German guards as having given him a cap. For this, Rivière spent 25 days in solitary confinement on bread and water. Out of pride and magnanimity, Rivière did not even record this in his diary and certainly held nothing against the poor Russian for having caused him to go through this ordeal.

When the Russians noticed that Rivière had long conversations with Teitelbaum, they felt it necessary to explain that the latter was not a real

Russian. They went on to enumerate grievances Russians had against Jews, especially the commercial exploitation of the masses. Although he never abandoned "the practical tolerance owed to his Western education, [Rivière] warmly espoused the side of the Russians." The Russians also alleged treason by the Jews in the 1905 Revolution, their "lack of understanding of the Russian heart." They also blamed the intelligentsia for its lack of concern for the masses, still essentially consisting of peasants interested in land. Then M[itzsenko?] and the Cossack attempted a lengthy psychological description of the Russians, at times comparing them to the French. Rivière recorded it with great interest.

> "The Russian people are good. The appearance may be coarse. But inside the soul is plain and good (*doucha prosta khorocha*). You cannot imagine it well here. You have seen us come to you only to beg. But before you judge our men, there is one thing you must think of: our men are hungry. They are not in their normal state. One cannot be normal when one is in that state. But deep down they are good.
>
> They do not know. But if one shows something to them, they learn. For example, regarding cleanliness, they may be dirty. But if you show them that it is better to wash, they do it."

> I reassured them immediately of my great sympathy for the Russian people. I told them that before the war I had a feeling for what they were like; that I was concerned with literature; that I had read their writers in French and that all that I had learned about their people had made me like them in advance, but since I knew them [firsthand] I liked them even more.

> That seemed to please them, and to surprise them a little also because of the recent episode[13] which I believe they remembered at the moment better than I.

> M. felt he had to answer me by expressing his opinion of the French. But what I liked is that he did so without flattering us and almost beginning with our faults, at least by expressing his initial impressions [of us], which were not of the most favorable kind.

> "It seems to me, he said in substance, that the French like each other and that there is even more unity among us. But at first, they behaved toward us almost as if they were enemies."

"The first evenings, when we prayed, the French remained seated, their hats on their heads and they would even hiss. I do not know what your beliefs are." At first I had not understood the last question. So K. who, speaking more distinctly, often served as our intermediary, translated thus: He asks if you are "an atheist or a fanatic." I answered that I was not "an atheist."

Then M. continued: "Well! I confess that the attitude of the French was painful (bolnò) to me. And there are things which I shall never forget.

But in the long run we got to know each other better. And we saw among you as everywhere good men and bad ones.

We who knew almost nothing, are so little educated, will have learned much here. One sees so many different people, of all races, one notices the way they behave with others. It is very interesting." (338-339)

Given the meaning he was to infer from the appearance of communism in Russia, it is useful to remember that as of November 28, 1916, Rivière had taken a stand on this question:

I felt how I was first of all an individualist, how individualism was for me the beginning of everything, and what incurable horror I felt towards this somber and monstrous doctrine [socialism] which postulates societies as anterior to individuals! (366)

March 14, 1917
Yesterday conversation with T[eitelbaum] on Dostoevsky.

I was telling him that in rereading *The Adolescent* I had the impression that I had been closer to him than now. Although he remains for me the greatest abyss of psychology and morality that I know, yet, because he is so unrestrained, he gives me at times the impression of going away whole, of evaporating in a sense. There is no center of gravity; nothing remains, holds, or pulls you back. The soul loses its weight in your hands. I am too well balanced now, too centered not to suffer from this dazzling flight. (In his works) one is as if carried away in too fast a carriage, the wind caused by the speed itself makes me suffocate and gives me a strange feeling of vacuum: I no longer feel myself. (405)

This is the expression by Rivière of a certain disappointment with Dostoevsky's works. It is based on the latter's technique which will ultimately be the object of Rivière's most severe criticism. Previously, however, he was to express his most lyrical praise for the Russian novelist. The same day, curiously, he resolved to compare himself to Dostoevsky:

"Resemblances and differences with Dostoevsky" (407). This led him first to a reflection on the purpose of literature.

> The true purpose of literature remains the expression of ideas and sentiments, of all this world which cannot be perceived otherwise. For where do they exist forming a whole, where else but in the expression which great writers give of it?
>
> What a joy yesterday to find again someone for whom the psychological world exists. (Rozanov: "Biographical Sketch," at the head of the *Complete Works* of Dostoevsky in the Marx edition, Saint Petersburg, 1894) (411)

And a page later:

> What I am lacking here is someone whom I could tell what God made of me, and who would understand how marvelous it is.[...] I do not know why I had made the impression last evening that this Rozanov, whose name I did not even know a moment earlier, would have understood me. I do not know why this sentence touched me:
>
> > "A crowd of listeners, such as only a thinker or a
> > painter could hope to have for himself, invisibly
> > and imperceptibly gathered...."
>
> I felt I was part of this crowd and in real exile here in a second sense, more cruel than the evident sense. Yet I was happy at the thought that I was a member of a society with them anyway, with the others over there, at the four corners of the world, who read and understand Dostoevsky.(412-413)

March 24, 1917

I regret now what I wrote on Dostoevsky the other day. Reading Rozanov's article yesterday, I felt that there was no one among the great writers to whom I was as close. And this morning, it seemed to me that I was called upon to produce something which would be like the counterpart of his work, with all the differences which correspond to our ethnic difference. It is an enormous ambition which I can avow only because I am alone. Besides, I said: the counterpart, not the equivalent.

Rozanov's preface touches me deeply. I have to translate it.[14] How it concerns me! How I understand what happened to me even better than before and throught it! (413)

Several days later he went on to quote Dostoevsky and Rozanov.

March 28, 1917

In spite of the hundreds of comrades around me, I lived in a terrible solitude and ended up cherishing this solitude.... I examined all my previous life. I judged it implacably and severely, and at times I blessed destiny for having sent me this solitude without which I could not have judged myself thus, nor gone over my past so strictly. (Dostoevsky: *The House of the Dead* quoted by Rozanov, p.XVI)

Rivière was also moved by Rozanov's sentence about Dostoevsky's stay in the penitentiary:

It is his soul that saved him when he was in the penitentiary, and not merely saved him, but made him wiser by purifying him of this crust which always forms in normal life on the surface of each of our souls.[15] (414)

He was comforted and reassured by the similarity he discovered between Dostoevsky's spiritual evolution while in the penitentiary and his own. It no doubt augmented his admiration for the Russian writer. This changed, however once he had been returned to a normal situation. Intensely hoping to be released soon, Rivière was eager to resume a normal life and above all to write. In this, he was again encouraged by Dostoevsky's precedent.

April 17, 1917

I was struck the other day by this sentence in Rozanov's preface: "The best half of his life was still ahead of him." I was struck, too, at the thought that Dostoevsky did not return from the penitentiary before he was 34 and was discharged from military service only at 39. And his entire work was written afterward. Therefore I, too, still have time.

What he [Dostoevsky] said on the choice of a career: how happy we were in that respect to have lived in a free country. The restriction against which he had to struggle: all white balls were needed merely to enter secondary school, etc. The energy lost in these ridiculous efforts....Anyway, now I understand that a "liberal regime" means something.

*

Will I dare note the analogies, which I discovered the other day between Dostoevsky's life and mine, while reading his biography.?

The son of a medical doctor, he had an austere, studious, and religious childhood. The country house. Lastly, the minute spent on the edge of death, and the penitentiary (I see all the differences well).

Still, he seemed to have lived long in a solitude of the mind which I have experienced only momentarily and to a degree. (416-417)

By the spring of 1917 even the prisoners of war were fairly abreast of the political upheaval which had begun to take place in Russia. This had become the main intellectual subject of discussion in the camps and had a considerable catalyzing influence on Rivière's political thought as well as on his opinion of the Russian people. At first, he greeted the Russian Revolution with joy because he felt that it would liberalize Russia. But by April 18, 1917, he had sensed a danger there for institutions he held dear.

The most recent events in Russia give me the impression, he wrote, that something so new, so terrible, so subversive for the English type of liberalism is already at work. And I do not mean to say that I sympathize more with that. But it is at last a third concept of values which appears among the ideas tossed about by the war, and it is perhaps the most redoubtable. (422)

He goes on to say that liberalism can no longer satisfy him and that he finds some of its aspects repugnant. He even briefly scorns

the freedom granted by liberals which can be used only to fight them. It is not ingratitude, it is logic.

That is why, I believe, I understand well what is happening in Russia at this time. The moment is solemn. For the first time in the world, a new ideal attempts to take shape... The question of socialism versus liberalism is doubled by the question of internationalism versus nationalism. (422)

Although a fierce nationalist in 1914 and although he still loved his country, Rivière had come to realize the enormous part nationalism had played in unleashing the war.

> Never doubtless more than now, he wrote, when we are tearing each other up, when national hatreds are most exacerbated, never have we been closer to establishing the United States of Europe. The sun rises in the Orient. And is it not naturally in Russia that it had to appear first, among the least formed people, the least actualized, consequently the least likely to impose them on others? I will also have to write down later everything that I find repugnant in those new values.

After having expressed his concern that the French are probably terribly unaware of what is happening and that they run the risk of being left out, he adds:

> Maybe it is nothing at all, nothing more than a new form of Russian disorder, of this weakness of the will, of this inability to "enter within" which characterizes Russians. But what if their very faults are in accord with the new values which are attempting to emerge and can serve them as support, as stem? What if perchance their turn had come? What if all of a sudden, in spite of our military virtues, our heroic obstinacy, we were about to be swept up--simply because times have changed, because a new epoch would have arrived? (423)

But Rivière was not only capable of having visionary flashes into the future and not of allowing himself to be carried away by a momentary idealism, he could also see quite realistically how difficult it would be for him to reconcile socialism with his background, his education, his normal way of life, and even his religious beliefs.

> April 20,1917
> No, I will not be diverted from the belief that this world is evil, that nothing can change it for the better, that suffering is in it as an immanent part of it, and that in whatever spot one may dig the soil to build on it, suffering gushes up as from a spring. No, I will not be separated from my dear brothers in thought, from Baudelaire, from Dostoevsky, from all the Christian thinkers. I will not fall among those reformers, those hygienists whom I have always hated even

before I understood what I held against them. I will believe
neither in Humanity, nor in the People, nor in Justice, nor in
Progress. These are but passing influences. Nor will the
course which events seem to be taking make me fall into
those heresies. And in spite of the efforts of internationalism, I will not believe that war could be banished from this
world. (424)

This passage is symptomatic of the depth and intensity of Rivière's religious belief to which he attempted logically to relate his philosophical
and political ideas. Given his state of mind, one can readily understand
his revulsion at the materialistic preoccupations on all sides.

What is disgusting to me in all political opinion, what prevents me from becoming emotionally involved in it, is the
fact that all deal only with material interests. Whereas, I
really believe I can say without bragging that I have no material interests. I only have spiritual interests.[...] Liberalism
[and] socialism, at bottom, are merely economic doctrines,
both pertaining only to the problem of food distribution.
Socialism wants all people to eat the same thing. Liberalism
wants those who eat better to continue to do so, and by way
of compensation it gives the others the right to vote, political
equality, that is to say the right to change this state of affairs
[...] if they can. (425)

On April 22, Rivière continued to develop his political reflection.

The extent to which [a political idea] can be exact or useful is indifferent to me; I only see what it wounds or disturbs.
Maybe my economic ideal is simply negative: the absence
of hunger, cold, dirt, ugliness for all. To guarantee such a
minimum, I can be interested. But beyond that, I find no interest in any positive acquisition. That is why on the one
hand I hate oppressive doctrines, those which more or less
hypocritically refuse to the wretched that which they need to
live free, but on the other hand I also hate all egalitarian
doctrines, those which formulate the ambitions of the
masses, their appetite for conquest.

It must be said: I find the world quite all right as it is. And
I may have some merit in saying it for I believe I am far from
being one of the profiteers; on the contrary, I have always
done all I could to do divest myself [of material possessions],
or at least I have never done anything to become rich.

I will also have to write down that which would appear irreparable, if the world such as it is were changed, if the socialist regime became established. (426)

Several times Rivière thought he understood what he liked and disliked about socialism. He tried again to summarize his position.

April 28, 1917
I believe I understand the exact nature of my feelings with respect to socialism and internationalism....These are values which are as remote as possible from my taste. But I see only too well the causes at work for their realization; and it is because I understand that I become attached to them. (434)

During the weeks which followed, Rivière continued to try to understand socialism better, and he attempted to imagine the changes and the consequences of its establishment on Western society, on France, as well as the logical philosophical and religious implications such a doctrine had for a Catholic such as he was. He came to the conclusion that the deep attraction socialism had for him was due to religious fervor and to foreign influence--especially to his sympathy for the Russians. At the same time, he felt great anguish for France:

May 10, 1917
And still now the need to do something, to run a risk of some sort for France, to prove well to myself and to others that it is not selfish interest that guides me in subscribing to the Russian thesis [socialism].

I am torn by two feelings, between which I am literally divided: the friendship for the Russians which nothing disturbs, which all the mockery addressed to them hurts, the approval of what they want to do—and on the other hand, my preference for my country, my attachment to all the good it holds in store for me, the need to see its interests triumph. I cannot come out of this [dilemma]. I can only suffer....Happy are the people whose sentiments are simple!...

I can see now that which I did not want to believe: that we have fought the war for capitalism. (444-445)

A week later, Rivière transcribed an entire page from Dostoevsky in Russian:

May 17, 1917

And there it is, my friend: the dusk of the first day of the European society I had dreamt about transformed itself for me as soon as I awakened into the last day of that same society. At that moment, it seemed as if one could hear the mournful knell toll over Europe. I do not mean to speak only of the war nor of the Tuileries; I knew without that that sooner or later all would pass, the whole face of the old European world; but I, Russian European, I could not tolerate it. Yes, they had just burnt the Tuileries...Oh! do not worry, I know that it was "logical." And I understand only too well the irrefutable character of the current idea, but as a representative of high Russian thought, I could not tolerate it, for high Russian thought encompasses all ideas. But who in the entire world would then have been capable of understanding such an idea: I was alone and wandering. I do not speak of myself personally but of Russian thought. Over there there was a struggle and logic; over there the Frenchman was only French, the German was only German, and that had never been truer during the course of their entire history; consequently, never did a Frenchman do as much harm to his "belle France" nor a German to his "Vaterland!"

In all of Europe then there was not a single European! I alone from among the incendiaries could tell them to their faces that burning the Tuileries was an error; I alone among all the conservative revenchards could shout that if their burning of the Tuileries was a crime, it was nevertheless a logical crime. And that, my boy, because I alone being Russian, was then in Europe the only European.[16] I do not speak of myself, I speak of all Russian thought. I was wandering, my friend, I was wandering and I knew very well that all that remained for me to do was to keep quiet and to wander... Yet, I felt sad. That is, my boy, because I cannot help respecting my nobility. (Dostoevsky: *The Adolescent*, Part III, Chap. 7). (447)

Rivière then analyzed this long passage, always attempting to situate himself with respect to Dostoevsky. At times, he contradicts himself in his pathetic search for clarity in his own ideas and for the best orientation to follow in the political and ideological chaos of Europe.

How disturbing to find these prophetic words of his,* and such a precise painting by him** of my present anguish! Or rather, of the sudden problem with which I grapple! For if I am sad, it is "as a Frenchman," and it is because I feel I am becoming a European. "All is sad to me" indeed at this time. I enter into a large country, empty of all that I had learned to love; I enter within the limits where I loved so much to feel that I was understood. I am cold, however, under this new sky without horizon, vast like that of Russia, like that of the world; and yet I must move on because my understanding is strong, impossible to withhold (and also my ideas).

But I am sad also at the same time and in the same way as he, and for the same reasons. I am sad over so much blood "logically" spilled! And I cannot prevent my thought from "wandering" and from grappling with all possible ideas. "I understand only too well the irrefutable character of the current idea." Did I not feel it well the other day, in that cruel minute when my comrades looked at me as one looks at a madman, and even a little as one looks at a traitor? (At that moment I shivered at the thought of what awaited me later, when I will have to tell the truth.) And yet, although I know now "that one must be quiet. It is *he** who told me, with this improbable, this almost diabolical divination which characterizes him. But, I am sad, oh! how sad I am, how "everything is sad to me" at this time!

I am so divided at this time that I can speak quite sincerely about the Russians as one must speak of them with the others and from our point of view, that is to say with contempt.[16] For I still feel this with the greatest force. The other is still merely abstract; but it grows with every instant and increasingly gains [ground] among my sentiments. I see now a new meaning in my love for Russia, which was so mysterious from the beginning. I understand the whole thought which Russia carries; the same seed which is in her must really have been placed in me, at the beginning, at my very birth. By what wind was it carried?

Is D[ostoevsky] sure that it is only as a Russian that he feels European? Is it not because Russia is oozing with Christianity? Was it not reported the other day in a news-

*"L'unique Européen."
**Dostoevsky

paper that some peasants refused to continue to fight because "it displeased Jesus?" (448-449)

After three years of meditation, Rivière had not sorted out his thoughts. He realized that within his political ideas there was a contradiction analogous to that which existed between his loves.

> I thought this morning that it was roughly the respective position of my two loves at the time I was writing the first chapter and epilogue of my novel.[17] It is now that of my patriotism and of my "europeanism." (449)

> May 19, 1917
> However, I will still write down this prophetic sentence of Dostoevsky's in spite of all that it implies: "Oh! it is not only the blood spilled then which frightened me so, it is not even the Tuileries, but all that was to follow. They were doomed to fight for still a long time because they are still too German and too French and as such they have not yet finished their action" (*The Adolescent*). (449-450)

Three weeks later, on June 14, Rivière was interned in Engelberg, Switzerland. He continued, irregularly, to record some of his thoughts in his notebooks. These reflections, however, no longer pertain directly to our subject.

NOTES

1   *L'Allemand, souvenirs et réflexions d'un prisonnier de guerre*, Paris: Gallimard, 1918.

2   *Aimée*, Paris: Gallimard, 1922.

3   This page number as well as all subsequent ones refer to J. Rivière's *Carnets (1914-1917)*, Paris: Fayard, 1974.

4   The prisoners were quartered in farm buildings.

5   Rivière wrote this name in Russian. Jacob Fediuk, Aphonin, Karol or K, Lavrov, Mitzsenko, Nickel and Teitelbaum were Russian prisoners of war whom Rivière knew in Koenigsbrück. No additional information could be found about them.

6   A French prisoner of war to whom Rivière makes numerous references.

7   Rivière had begun studying Russian just a few days earlier. Here he meant to transcribe the Russian name for "b," the "soft sign."

8   A French fellow prisoner-of-war.

9   Rivière's three-year-old daughter.

10   This appears to be a phonetic transcription of *Dresdener Depesche* as pronounced in Russian by Fédiouk.

11   *Komu*: for whom, or who's next?

12   Recorded in English by Rivière.

13   The episode referred to is about the cap given to the Russian who tried to escape and which landed Rivière in solitary confinement for 25 days.

14   Rivière never kept this resolution and actually no translation of Rozanov's "preface" has appeared. W. Edward Brown has recently translated it and it will appear in *The Russian Tri-Quarterly*.

15   The two passages above are quoted by Rivière in Russian.

16   The French felt betrayed, when under the impact of their Revolution, the Russians decided to sue for peace with the Central Powers.

17   *Aimée.*

III. THE RUSSIANS REAPPRAISED (1917 - 1925)

1. Rivière's Disillusionment with the Russians (1917-1925)

Rivière was demobilized in January 1919. For the following six months he was preoccupied with securing the directorship of the *Nouvelle Revue Française* whose secretary he had been before the war. Soon he was absorbed by the review, which resumed publication in July 1919. But he continued to follow events in Russia closely. In the September 1919 issue of the *N. R. F.* he published his first major post-war article which was essentially inspired by the Russian Revolution. The essay is entitled "*Décadence de la liberté* ".[1] It is divided into two parts. In the first Rivière reminds his readers that the war had been fought primarily for "law and freedom." He laments ironically that not only had the notion of justice not been sharpened, but that "available freedom far exceeded demand." He felt political upheavals in central and eastern Europe, especially in Russia, meant that people were of their own accord forsaking their freedom or neglecting to claim it although it had been paid by the sacrifice of millions.

Rivière used Russia as an example of a country where freedom had been deliberately abandoned in exchange for totalitarian socialism. In attempting to explain the appearance of communism there, he relied on his understanding of the Russian personality such as he had discovered it through art, language, and prolonged contact with Russians. Such an approach had its limitations--those of deductive logical reasoning versus the frequent unpredictability and gratuity of events. Basing his argument on his own preference for liberalism, wishful thinking made him write that communism as such had no chance of remaining permanently established in Russia. He thought he did understand why it began there. He saw it as a consequence of the Russians' propensity for collectivism, but he felt they were too humane to tolerate it very long.

Rivière wrote that the democracies had not fought the war only to remain free themselves but also to enable other peoples to attain freedom. He felt the war was in the tradition of the French Revolution which had as one of its ideals the emancipation of peoples. To his amazement and deep disappointment, he realized that collectivism, oppression, and surveillance were being institutionalized in place of freedom. He was most aggrieved by these developments in Russia and her empire. Before he attempted again at least a partial explanation of the Russian character which he no longer considered to be simple and naïve, he was most discouraged and disillusioned when he wrote the introduction to his article:

> I do not presume to have penetrated to the bottom of the
> Russian soul, the most difficult, the most secret, the most
> disappointing there is. I feel that in its essence it remains for-
> ever unfathomable, just as its language is just about im-
> possible for a foreigner to master. (*N.R.F.* XII, 511)

Then he proceeded to paint a rather unflattering portrait of the Russians in which he even included old *clichés* about their orientalism.

> Even his genial traits are fleeting and Oriental. He who
> might have thought he had apprehended them is cheated.
> No people is more deceiving and cheating than the Russians
> even on the psychological level. (*N.R.F.* XII, 51)

As we shall see, here he was beginning to include Dostoevsky among those who disappointed him. He was already alluding to a notion which he was later to develop, that Dostoevsky had the art of taking his reader to the deepest psychological abyss, but without enlightening him about it--thus deceiving him.

In 1919, Rivière felt that the French had no reason to believe that their former allies shared their ideals, their love of freedom. It then appeared to him that the difference between the French and the Russians as well as between their respective civilizations was considerable. He now felt that an earlier realization of this fact would have spared his countrymen a ridiculous and almost tragic error—that of foolishly choosing their allies. He then explained the psychological basis for the Russians' development of the soviet system. Even in very crowded prison camp barracks, the French were determined to preserve at least a parcel of privacy in which to shelter their individuality. Not so with the Russians, wrote Rivière:

> They spontaneously lived in a state of agglomeration.
> They formed one group, as if they were a school of fish. They
> chattered like a nestful of birds. Even their arguments lacked
> seriousness [...] Theirs are astonishingly little-retrenched
> souls....Among them the individual is without weight; his
> insufficient density forces him to dread shocks, it prevents
> him from asserting himself. He asserts himself only through
> tenderness, complaint, ruse or treason. (*N.R.F.* XII, 513)

In their tendency to congregate, Rivière saw a partial explanation for the Russians' alleged individual weakness and lack of bravery. Since to him freedom had to be won and defended in dire struggles, he felt the Russians were not ready for it.

So much timidity prevented the Russian from having any
desire, any will for individual emancipation. It is not with a
tender but unsteady heart that he could wish for freedom
and for the right to do what he would want. Nothing could
be stranger to this sensitive and weak being than our hard
ideal of independence and work. (*N.R.F.* XII, 513-14)

Here he did not contrast the Russian with the Frenchman, but with the
Englishman, capable of standing alone and whom he regarded as the
Russian's most exact antithesis (*N.R.F.* XII, 516). To this weakness in
his character, he also attributed the Russian's alleged lack of initiative.
He regarded personal initiative as a manifestation of individuality. The
Russians' mysterious propensity to come together results in mass movements as opposed to individual initiative. Thus he saw the organization
of their society in *soviets* as a natural consequence of their accession to
the freedom of organizing, which they momentarily had after the downfall of the tsar's regime. He felt that the *soviet* was the system which corresponded most to the temperament of the people and that they could
be freed from it only through outside interference (*N.R.F.* XII, 522).
"Bolshevism is the barely organized and systematized blossoming of the
Russian's [propensity for collectivism]" (*N.R.F.* XII, 519). And whereas it might go against weak and individual wills, it flatters the Russian's
strong need to exercise power collectively. Aside from the psychological
compatibility Rivière saw between the Russians and socialism, he was
well aware of the consequences of the Revolution in Russia.

Even if it is true that the Russian people now endure horrible miseries, even if they repent for being bolshevik, the
fact remains that through them on a point of the globe, socialist existence has begun. (*N.R.F.* XII, 522)

Half a year after this most severe of Rivière's criticisms of the Russians, in March 1920, he wrote about the performance of Diaghilev's
ballet company at the Paris Opera House. First, he correctly remarked
that the company had already severed its ties with Russia prior to the
war and that it assimilated whatever substance it had been able to gather
abroad. Thus its art no longer was purely Russian.

We are rather far now from those full and harmonious
successes whose names were: *Prince Igor, Petrushka, The
Rite of Spring.* We must frankly say it: over is the time when
all our senses, when our very heart at once found in Russian
Ballet a refreshing and delectable potion. Only our curiosity
still remains attached.[2]

140

In his eyes Stravinsky remained a "prodigious musican," and his *Petrushka,* and *Rite of Spring* were still the only two really great works to have appeared since *Pelléas.*

For over a year, Rivière did not express his feelings on either the Russians or their art. In fact, he seemed to have become either distracted from the new situation or reconciled to it--after all, the Communists were by then confined to their borders by the policy of the *"cordon sanitaire."* In any case, his very short article, published in May 1921 on the performance of *"Le Choeur ukrainien"* is cordial if brief. As if trying to convince himself that he could not sulk about the Russians forever, he wrote, "It will not be easy for us to replace the Russians, nor even the Ukrainians."[3] The memory of the numerous recitals he had heard as a prisoner of war and the naïveté in Mussorgsky which originally had moved him and captured his imagination were again having their magic effect.

For the three years preceding his death in February 1925, Rivière led an extremely busy life as editor of the most prestigious French literary review — the *Nouvelle Revue Française,* as political journalist (writing for the *Luxemburger Zeitung*), as novelist, and as critic (enthusiastically explicating Marcel Proust, Paul Valéry, and Sigmund Freud). Since the Soviet Union was isolated from the rest of the world, Rivière had few if any occassions to document himself and write on subjects pertaining to contemporary Russian culture.

As editor of the *Nouvelle Revue Française*, he did, however, publish a special issue in honor of Dostoevsky's centennial in 1922. Although it is not known whether this homage volume was undertaken on his initiative or at Gide's suggestion, Rivière did contribute a short essay to it entitled "On Dostoevsky and the Unfathomable."[4] This essay is not dithyrambic praise, as is all too often the case on such occassions, but lucid and incisive criticism. Henri Peyre in 1960 still regarded this short essay as "one of the most acute critiques formulated in Western Europe of the most Russian of novelists."[5] Rivière's basic premise is that a novelist "may either want to produce full darkness or he may want to eliminate it for the reader." These two approaches appeared to him as typical of Dostoevsky and of French novelists respectively. He wrote that Dostoevsky "is primarily interested in [psychological] abysses and it is in suggesting that it is quite impossible to fathom these depths that he succeeds," whereas French novelists, when faced with complexity, try to organize and elucidate it while depicting it.[6] Thus they do not give the feeling of vertigo in the contemplation of the human soul. Reversing his stand as stated in *"Le Roman d'aventure,"* Rivière thought in 1922 that Dostoevsky's method was not supreme. He felt "an abyss means nothing as long as one has not descended into it and explored it"

(*N.R.F.* XVII, 177). He also argued against the inconsistencies of some of Dostoevsky's characters. Depth and consistency can coexist in a character, he felt, because every human being is its own logical system. At this time, Rivière no longer saw Dostoevsky as the inimitable master novelist. In the last paragraph of his essay, he outlined the possible tasks of a new novelist superior to the "adventurous genius Dostoevsky," creator of the depths (*N.R.F.* XVII, 178).

His criticism was truly original in its severity. After a lyrical evocation of the time of his boundless admiration for Dostoevsky, he focused his attention on three points. He did not like to admit, however, that it was criticism of Dostoevsky, claiming that he simply needed

> to react against the writer and especially against his psychological method—or better against those who would want to present it as the only one capable of leading us to extreme depths.[7]

He went on to explain that if Dostoevsky remains insufficiently known, it is because of his technique, which "consists in discovering abysses, whereas we [the French] endeavor to explore abysses." Rivière is representative of the French when he writes that the task of the novelist is "to give a complex but coherent representation of souls." Though also realizing the shortcomings of the French technique, as a true son of Descartes and Comte, he presented it as being superior to that of Dostoevsky.

> It is quite evident that there is an apparent incoherence in our actions, a superficial dispersion of our conscience, a contradiction among our immediate moments. But there is also logic of the character, which the ultimate goal of psychology may well to be find and to reveal.[8]

This was not a new attitude toward Dostoevsky's method. Even in the spring of 1917, when he was perhaps spiritually closest to him, when he was dumbfounded by his prophetic visions of the future of Europe, he had reservations about the Russian novelist's creative process. Whereas on March 23 he experienced a quasi-mystical exhilaration at the thought of being "anyway a member of the universal society of those who read and understand Dostoevsky," the next day he wrote:

> I regret now what I wrote the other day on Dostoevsky. Reading Rozanov's article[9] yesterday, I felt I was not as close to any of the great writers [as I was to Dostoevsky]. And this morning, it seemed to me I had the calling to produce something which would be the counterpart of his work

with all the differences which correspond to our ethnic difference. [This is an] enormous ambition which I dare confess only because I am alone. Besides, have said: the counterpart, not the equivalent. (*Carnets,* 413)

He remained fascinated by the similarities between his life and that of Dostoevsky's and on April 3, he could not resist the temptation to list them:

Will I dare note the analogies which I discovered the other day reading his biography, between his life and mine?

He was the son of a doctor. He had an austere, hardworking and religious youth. There was the house in the country. Finally the minute on the edge of death, the prison (though I do realize there were differences)! (*Carnets,* 417)

The greatest similarity he had noticed earlier. They both saw salvation as possible only through suffering. This concept had enabled Rivière to accept his captivity without despair and regard it in fact as a providential means of saving his soul. He was probably never more religious than during his captivity. Already in 1915 he recalled how fortunate he was for having been imprisoned with Russians. He was convinced life was bearable for him in the camp thanks to their presence. Rivière never denied this similarity on the spiritual plane and his mystical kinship with Dostoevsky. He recalled it when he wrote his article on Dostoevsky in 1922, though with melancholy and nostalgia, for he then no longer lived on as high a spiritual level and no longer even thought of emulating his former spritual mentor. Not without deep regret, to be sure, as the beginning of the unpublished first draft of his article reveals:

Why should I not confess how I sobbed the day André Gide revealed Dostoevsky to me by reading for me the chapter in *The Brothers Karamazov* which tells of the martyrdom and the death of the "offended" Aliosha? Maybe I shall never encounter another writer who will be as disturbing and with as loving a heart. For years Dostoevsky was for me quasi-eucharistic nourishment. I took him each day to help my faith, to sustain my charity. He appeared to me as the greatest revealer of [psychological] depth, and he gave me a feeling of vertigo before [the mystery] of the human soul.

I am not very proud of the changes which have occurred in my spirit and in my heart, and which have put a distance between him and me. Maybe I will always consider the time I spent in his intimacy as the best of my life.[10]

In 1922, Rivière undoubtedly continued to admire Dostoevsky's *"grandeur d'âme."* In his essay he merely criticized his approach to the exploration of psychological mysteries. At that time, his personal spiritual evolution was probably much more responsible for his estrangement from Dostoevsky than the changes wrought by the Russian Revolution. As his main link with Russian culture in general, Dostoevsky through his spiritual mediation could have mitigated Rivière's great disillusionment with the Russians.

*

Between 1815 and 1917, Russia underwent many profound changes which until the outbreak of the Bolshevik Revolution tended to bring her increasingly in line with Western European cultures. This evolution, however, was not perceived, nor did it really interest artists such as Rivière who were prepared to adhere to an archaic and romanticized image of Russia. Like many others, he was influenced by the then prevalent anthropological and poetic notion regarding the roots of human civilization, which were thought to be found in Asia, "our *alma mater*," as Rivière explained. Coincidentally, the Russian music and even the literature with which he familiarized himself and which he appreciated before the war allowed him to entertain such a romanticized vision. In this, Rivière's perception of the Russian personality was typical of a French or indeed of a Western intellectual of his time. It changed, however, during his prolonged contact with Russian prisoners during the war. Paradoxically, it did not lead him to a better comprehension of the Russian personality. True, both he and the Russians were in circumstances which were far from typical or ideal. During his captivity Rivière became fervently religious and patriotic as well as deeply attached to Western liberalism. This explains that military and other consequences of the Russian Revolution caused him to react negatively and to make his most sweeping and perhaps most unfair generalizations. It is also in the wake of this disappointment with Russians that he made his severe although defensible reassessment of Dostoevsky. Thus if Rivière's criticism of Russian music and of Dostoevsky remains valid on the whole, his remarks on and his analyses of the elusive and changing personality of the Russian people often seem questionable-- not for lack of sympathy, but before 1917 because of prevalent archaic anthropological notions and later because his vision of the frightful psychological, social, and cultural consequences of collectivism.

NOTES

1   *N.R.F.*, XII (September, 1919), pp. 498-522.

2   "Ballets Russes à l'Opéra, etc..." *N.R.F.*, XIII (March 1920), p.463.

3   "Le Choeur ukrainien,..."*N.R.F.*, XV (May 1981), pp.626-27.

4   The February 1922 issue of the *N.R.F.* was dedicated to Dostoevsky to commemorate the centennial of his birth.

5   *The Ideal Reader, Selected Essays by Jacques Rivière,* edited and translated by Blanche A. Price with a preface by Henri Peyre, New York, Meridian Books, 1960.

6   "De Dostoïevski et de l'insondable," *N.R.F.*, XVII (February 1922), pp.175-176.

7   Rivière's criticism is even harsher in the manuscript draft which was made available to me by his son, Alain Rivière, and from which this passage is quoted.

8   *Ibid.*

9   Vasili E. Rozanov. Rivière is referring to and at times paraphrasing Rozanov's introduction to *Polnoe sobranie Socinenij F. M. Dostoevskogo. Tom pervyj, chast' pervaja.* S-Petersburg: Izdanie A. F. Marksa, 1894.

10   Quoted from the unpublished draft. See footnote 7.

2. Rivière's Writings in Reaction to
His First-Hand Assessment of Russians
and to Communism

Russia[1]
by Jacques Rivière

April 1916.[2] The dificulty in general of understanding foreigners. Difficulty especially for a Frenchman. Why? Because he has a very neat and set character. Thus he has no doubts. His taste, his judgement are the good ones. There is no need to look any further. All one needs to do is to see him here.[3] He is the norm, and not once will the idea that he could not be the norm occur to him. From the way he fries his potatoes down to his theater, it is what he does that constitutes the norm. More is involved here than the attachment to national mores and institutions which one finds in every people; there is a tendency to universalize them.

It is at the same time sublime and odious. For it indeed corresponds to a true superiority. It is the feeling of an ancient dignity, of a regal people. In most cases, what France has contributed to other countries has proved to be good. And peoples have often been in need of its laws.

But it is also odious. For there is also something else besides France. There is no point in denying this fact, for it could lead to regrettable clashes.

Even without going so far, a Frenchman almost always has an unpleasant attitude while abroad. All great travelers agree that a Frenchman is boring on a trip. He is not sufficiently respectful. He has taken with him all his little ideas; he has his standard set in advance by which to measure all that he finds. He never hesitates.[4]

In order to understand foreigners, a certain shyness in necessary. One must not be so sure at first that one is right. One must be awkward and not know how to go about things, be searching, groping, willing to conform, and therefore be forced to adapt.

Even more is needed: some prior belief in the diversity of human nature, in the possibility of multiple fulfillment for the human being.

On this point there are two opposed tendencies between which one must keep his place. The classical thesis coming from Antiquity: man is the same everywhere and always. The modern thesis: man does not exist; there are only races or even individuals. Montaigne. Quotation from Gobineau. Introduction to *Nouvelles Asiatiques*, p.4, sq.[5]

To me, Gobineau's thesis seems as false as the other. It seems to me that in order to demonstrate the extreme diversity among men, he leans too much on moral differences, for morality is itself merely a product. The cause is psychological. And quite opposite results can come from a very small difference in the cause. Differences in colors in ceramics are produced by a slight difference in dosage. Similarly, certain very close character traits can result in opposite behavior. Disparities are amplified by divergences.

The relative unity of human nature is especially evident to whoever has once noticed that defects and qualities can have the same origin, can come from the same fold in the mind or heart. Psychological unity precedes and produces moral diversity.

Here, as always in science, there is a middle ground which properly speaking is the scientific attitude. One ought not to generalize too soon but wait, let diversity occur before looking for uniformity. Our French tendency to universalize will always be strong enough. We can [afford to] go against it all the way. I see how a deeper understanding of the science of man is possible only through us, and to the extent that we will repress our temperament. After Stendhal's magnificent discoveries.... We should allow ourselves to be classical only perforce. We shall always be classical enough.

Let us return to our subject. In order to understand foreigners, one must combine two attitudes: one must first consider him as a foreigner, that is to say as different from oneself, and then be ready to find oneself in him.

And then finally and above all one has to have a little curiosity, love, and be capable of forgetting oneself. One must believe that other thoughts and feelings than one's own cannot only exist but also be loveable.

Yet, even with the best disposition, there is something difficult to understand in the Russian character. It is a kind of infinity. To define that which is undefinable in the Russian. Something which is not too complex, for there is a rather remarkable uniformity over such a vast territory, but something which is too large, impossible to circumscribe, to grasp.

There are political movements which begin, but which are impossible to follow to their end: at a certain point our attention leaves us without our realizing it. Thus we know this or that happened at a given time. But what resulted from it?

It is an empire which is still looking for its borders and is still trying to absorb more in order to find them. That is the source of the Russian spirit of conquest.

With all that happens in Russia, with all that is Russian, it is always as if there were an open door behind, and what begins here ends only beyond:

"Even well fed, the wolf always looks to the forest; even while coming closer to Europe, Russia is always looking toward Asia.[6]

And yet, Russia is not the Orient; she is simply open to the Orient; Russia escapes there when we want to grasp her....And she receives echoes from here. Here we should speak of music—the difference between a song of the island of Chios and *The Polovtsian Scenes*, for example. But that is only an escape hatch. It is a negative trait in the Russian character. This corresponds to a certain lackadaisical, dreamy attitude, to the propensity for infinity in their thought. Gogol's passage on Russia in Canto XI of *Dead Souls*.[7]

Nevertheless, this infinity makes communication difficult with us. It is as if Russia were ill at ease in presenting herself to the West. She does not know where to seek her identity, how to gather herself together for us. And that is why she resorts to a government which properly speaking is not national. She is forced to borrow elements from the West, especially from countries with which she comes into contact in order to establish relations with the West. Her unity, her mark (a necessary thing in any act or intervention), she is forced to have made abroad.. And that is an additional difficulty, for she thus presents herself with a face which is not her own. And those who would take it as an expression of her inner essence would completely miss the point.

If, however, we cannot hope to understand Russia, let us at least try to touch her. Let us recognize several centers, several points of convergence, several groups of characters; I do not say qualities and faults can very well form groups, blend under a same title.

And this is not an apology of Russia that we are trying to make but a portrait. When we love someone, it is not because he is perfect. His faults and his good qualities have a similar color and it is this color that we love. In order to move progressively, let us begin by a trait which is related to the infinity against which we stumbled first.

It is extremely difficult to grasp because it is dual. It is the union of vivacity, neatness, precision, and infinity.

There is an infinity which consists in lack of definition: it introduces some play into everything, it blows up all details and drowns them. Everything becomes inflated with sights and aspirations like someone who has bubbles in the stomach. This infinity is not what gives a religious character to thought. There is nothing undetermined about religion, and religious feeling is not a feeling of want. Quite the contrary. It is much rather the feeling of a fact, an unimpeachable datum.

Russian infinity is of another kind. It does not encroach upon one's character, it does not drown it. From the midst of the liveliest, the most active precision there are great and sudden vistas; it is a gushing infinity.

The southern aspect of Russian thought. Already in the language there are many related sounds. Look at the faces. Many are coarse; none is heavy.

Music: the admirable babbling of the children's room, Mussorgsky's minute and myriad speech. The language reminds one of a nestful of birds which chirp and tease each other with little blows of the beak.

The distance which creates mystery as in Ibsen.

Infinity suddenly bursts out in these so lively hearts. It is a new vivacity, an impatience, a frenzy which cannot be contained any longer, a sudden and boundless caprice.

We said that we would but touch the Russian genius without grasping it. Let us take then another point without worrying about the connection.

The French exist in an individual state before they exit in a societal state. One could say the opposite of the Russians. The groups they form around a stove. A kind of community, of an initial confusion from which differences emerge, but only after resemblances. All the stems are in the same soil. This is very striking in Dostoevsky. The social state in which all his characters are. The conversations. They have to be together for life to be born in them and for their individual being to awaken. *The Possessed.*

Of course the French are not all different from one another. But they begin as if they were. Each has his little personality, his head, his haircut. And if perchance he resembles another, it is as a type. It is a little annoying sometimes to find this toylike perfection, this somewhat curtailed fulfillment. All the difficulties in the history of France come from the necessity of getting these little cocks to live together without pecking each other.

I do not know the functioning of Russian communes. But I can see very well on what character trait this organization rests. They are people for whom community is anterior to its elements. This is an extremely ancient trait, if I am to believe the *Sacre du Printemps.*

The beauty of the choruses. Nowhere are they as perfect. The way they settle in one another's place, on top of one another. Tenants and sub-tenants: the little corner. People grafting themselves on one another.*(The Honest Robber, The Basement.)*

In sum, Natorp[8] was right: it is a people still held in a matrix of homogeneity, with differentiation hardly begun. The only difference is that he sees in this a phase in time, whereas I believe that it is an eternal psychological trait which is no doubt subject to development, but which will always remain. For it is not natural that, just as one people is called upon to play and personify all the nuances of individualism, another is, on the contrary, responsible for modulating social life.

The proof of it is in the form of the language. A continuous scale of vowels. All the intermediate sounds and for each sign the possibility of oscillating between two poles. Similarly, nothing is fixed in the language. Substantives and adjectives can be multiplied by their diminutives. The verbs: the way they help each other, they cannot do anything one without the other; their solidarity, their gregariousness. And it is not only in pairs that they go. But in addition to the frequentative and the one which expresses an isolated action, there is a continuity from the original verb to the derivative; for certain derivatives are used to express certain tenses or aspects of the original verb, and thus there is no break between their roles as auxiliaries and the moment when they decidedly assume another meaning as derivatives. This is a morphological process: epenthesis or philological grafting. This is the exact reflection of the cohabitation I have spoken of. Extraordinary hospitality for words: they are always hosting someone; and they often disappear under their guests.

No doubt one could say that it is a language which is as yet unfinished. But that is of course not the case. Just think: how could it become finished? It would have to change its character in order to attain the definition of morphological and syntactic individualism. In order to permit the establishment of general rules, principally as far as verbs are concerned, it would be necessary for the language to give up its fundamental process. Each verb would have to become emancipated and find within itself all the necessary forms to express the different tenses. But then what would happen to the others which used to express the tenses for which up to now it has been insufficient? They would have to disappear, to perish. It would be therefore a complete revolution in the language, with all the throat-cutting which is usual in times of revolutions; this would therefore be entirely different from a flowering.

I am coming to a trait which derives from the preceding, but which also introduces us to the greatest depth of the Russian character, to the aspect by which it is most disconcerting to us. I am grateful to T.[9] for having called my attention to it.

First point: just as the very clear demarcation between individuals develops and enhances the feeling for ownership, so does communal life weaken it. The human being who is alone and different rapidly becomes accustomed to consider all that belongs to him by a sacred tie. That forms a world with him. On the contrary, the other does not feel that it is a part of his substance. It is something absolutely adventitious, detachable, trasferable in one way as well as in the other.

From this one can derive at once a good quality and a fault of the Russians. First their incontestable generosity without ulterior motive. Their ability to strip themselves entirely, truly without thinking about themselves or about their needs and with respect to the person to whom one gives. The Frenchman always gives with the thought of the effect that this will produce; this reinforces in him his feeling of superiority. On the contrary, the Russian gives to the poor as one gives to God. True charity. The beggar is truly the image of Jesus Christ. Very beautiful passage by Tolstoy in *On Life*. He gives because really the riches of this world are only rot for him, and because he who is deprived of them is the saint *par excellence* and from this fact alone he receives an exceptional kind of dignity. One can see how this idea is opposed to ours, but how close it is to the Evangelical concept: wealth is an obstacle, the great obstacle, the mountain which hides everything. At bottom, all of Tolstoy can be reduced to this idea.

Together with this weakness of the notion of ownership in the Russians there is their readiness to steal and their corruptibility. Just as they can easily strip themselves, so do they easily strip others. Stealing is not the sacrilege it is for us. (This morning, I heard a Frenchman say: "For stealing, there is no punishment too great!") And indeed this is quite natural, given our individualistic conception. But it may not be God's opinion: the thieves. Corruptibility seems to be the counterpart of disdain for wealth. Here, however, one must look at the matter from the point of view I indicated: a defect often is only the parody of a good quality instead of being its negation. The initial psychological trait here is not contempt for property but a weakness of the notion of property. And to give easily and not to resist being given to are two ways of not thinking about it very strongly.

Let us examine here for ourselves this feature of the Russian character and try really to penetrate into the foreign soul and learn from what we find in it. Is there an example for us to extract from it? It is of course out of the question of individual taking back, etc. [sic]. These are theories in which esteem, in the absence of respect for property, is strictly implied.

But without going either through a Christian apology of poverty and without taking too sharp a position, let us ask ourselves if a reduction of the preoccupation with wealth by cultivated minds would not have immense repercussions. The habit of trying to always have as much as possible. Acquiring even when it is not necessary, by impulse, out of duty. There is no question of disregarding the considerable differences which wealth makes, nor even to deny that it is a condition of the development of liberalism. (Jealousy soils everything among the poor.) But, my God, how easy life is without wealth, or at least without perpetually thinking of acquiring or augmenting it. If one could divert one's eyes from the greater part of this hallucinating object! If one could relax the grip of this hand of steel which grips the world. Actually, as long as one has enough to keep clean, to afford the little bit of fancy which is like the flower of life, the rest is unimportant. It is not wisdom, or renunciation of what one could not obtain. What I ask for is lightness of heart and trust in the future. I am not speaking here to the wretched. I would speak to them in an entirely different way. For I would be ashamed of seeming to take their destitution lightly. But to those who are spared the great necessity of brutalizing work from morning till evening, to all those who already enjoy a little freedom. And I do not ask them to moderate their desires, but to see their happiness and to embrace it on the spot and no longer allow themselves to be a mean, stubborn, relentless, furious, and narrow-minded beast caught between the shafts of greed and ambition.

Nothing annoys me as much as Franklin. Really, what genius is there in economizing? It can be proposed as a commercial or industrial example, but not as a model for individual morality. Really, how can a man be better for having filled up his piggy bank little by little? What beauty, what moral greatness is there in that? There is patience. To how many more fruitful labors could it have been employed? I prefer the Russian functionary who will piously let himself be handed several thousand rubles which tomorrow he will cast to the winds.

But I am saying too much. Let us suppose I simply wanted to recommend making: ah! a little sigh whereby quite simply the heavy dream of wealth will suddenly vanish and leave you so peacefully awakened!

NOTES

1   "Russia" was first published in *Le Roseau d'Or*, Oeuvres et Chroniques No. 14, 1927 and reprinted in *Le Français* (Paris: Aveline, 1928), 135-156.

2   These notes were written in captivity by Jacques Rivière, as well as all those which form the first part of *A la trace de Dieu*, to serve as a basis for the lectures he gave before a small group of comrades. One should therefore seek in them only the schema of his thought which here abruptly leaves its subject and deviates toward a moral question, and then stops short. But this thought is so vigorous that at every moment it explodes the narrow limits of the plan and bursts into truth so acute and at the same time so simply satisfying that by this virtue it appeared worthy to us of being offered to the reader, though the garb under which it is presented may be summary and without finish.—I[sabelle] R[ivière, the author's wife who published from 1925 to 1971 many of the manuscripts he had left.]

3   At the prisoners' camp at Königsbrück.

4   One must take exception with Rivière on this point, especially since Frenchmen today do not behave in this fashion although they continue to be quite ironic. Not only did he exaggerate, but what Rivière regarded as a French trait is in fact an attitude commonly observed in the nationals of any powerful country. Englishmen were disliked for their smugness, until the discomfiture of their empire, the Germans for their arrogance whenever powerful, and in similar circumstances have we not been called ugly Americans?

152

5   "Contrary to what moralists teach, men are nowhere the same. One can easily see that a Chinese has two arms and two legs, two eyes and a nose like an Hottentot or a Parisian, but one does not have to speak one hour with each of them to notice and to conclude that there are no intellectual or moral ties between them, except for the conviction that one must eat when hungry and sleep when sleepy. On all other subjects, on the manner by which to gather ideas, the nature of these ideas, the way they cross-fertilize each other, the way they blossom, their colors, everything is different. For the black south of the Tchad lake, it is reasonable, indispensable, praiseworthy, pious to massacre the foreigner as soon as he can be caught; and if one wrings the last breath out of his body by means of finely graduated, modulated, and applied torture, so much the better, and the operator's conscience will feel marvelous for it. Let the same foreigner fall into the hands of an Egyptian Arab, the latter will have no peace, no contentment until one way or another he will have wrung his last penny from him and if possible stripped him of his shirt. The Black and the Arab assuredly disagree on the way to treat humanity. But imagine them in a dialogue with St. Vincent de Paul. What will the common ground be between these three natures? If a moralist is introduced as judge of the discussion, do you think that he will be able to maintain, as he would have done until then, that men are the same everywhere? Logically, of course not; in fact, he will not fail to do so, in order to make his system triumph and for the sake of simplicity." [J.R.]

6   A Russian proverb as quoted by J.R.

7   O Russia! Russia! From the far-away places where I reside I see you, poor, hard, and inhospitable land where none of the marvels of art are added to those of nature in order to cheer or frighten one's gaze. One looks in vain on your land for those cities with splendid palaces hanging over precipices, those ivy-covered houses where in the roar of foamy cascades colorful trees are hanging; one need not throw one's head back in order to contemplate blocks of stone piled up to dazzling heights; one does not see through a row of dark arches hanging with vine-branches, ivy and wild roses, the unchanging lines of mountains etched out brilliantly upon the silvery sky. Solitude in uniformity, that is what you offer everywhere; like imperceptible points, your low cities blend with the plains. But what secret force draws me to you? Why does the plaintive song which vibrates from sea to sea in your vast expanse ceaselessly resound in my ears? What is the meaning of this sobbing call which grips one's soul? What sounds insinuate themselves like painful caresses into my heart and obsess it continually? Russia, what do you want of me? Why are you looking at me like this? Why does all that you hold turn eyes full of expectation toward me?

...While I remain puzzled and motionless, a threatening cloud, ready to burst with rain, darkens the sky above me, and my thought remains dumb in the presence of its immensity. What does this incommensurable expanse portend? Unlimited, will you not give birth to a genius as vast as you are? Are you not predestined to bear heroes, you who offer so much space for them to try themselves? Your powerful hugeness fills me with enthusiasm, disturbs me to the very depth of my being; a supernatural force opens my eyes. O Russia, land of sparkling horizons, sublime, unknown to the rest of the earth!... (T. 1, p.396 of the Bossard edition.)

8   A modern German philosopher [J.R.]. Rivière had read his works and referred to him in his controversial *L'Allemand*, Gallimard, 1918.

9   Most likely Teitelbaum, a Russian prisoner of war who, however, was originally from Poland.

Decadence of Freedom[1]
by Jacques Rivière

I do not presume to have penetrated to the bottom of the Russian
soul. It is the most difficult, the most secret, the most disappointing. I
think that in its essence it remains forever inaccessible, just as its language is almost impossible for a foreigner to master. There is a Russian
proverb which says: "Whatever you feed a wolf, it always looks towards
the forest." As far as Russia advances to meet Europe, it still remains
completely turned toward Asia. And indeed, one has the impression
that its genius escapes through this immense opening toward the East
each time one thinks to have captured it. I say it without hate, but there
is no more guileful people than the Russians, even from the psychological point of view: what they leave you with is almost always "holding
the bag."

There are, however, some very evident traits in their character which,
well observed, well followed, would have enabled us to foresee how few
their reasons were for falling in love with freedom, and to [discover] in
the service of what a completely different ideal they were fatefully going
to employ their might. With a little insight we would have avoided the
almost ridiculous disappointment their revolution has caused.

I recall having had, from the very first moments of my captivity, the
direct feeling of what I shall call the *soviet* phenomenon.

The Germans had gathered us together with the Russians and distributed equal numbers of us in each barrack. It was, they said, so that
we might learn to know "our dear allies," in other words, to become
disgusted with them. So we lived side by side, or rather on top of one
another, for we were so tightly packed that ideally in the evening we
should have gone to bed all at the same time; whoever came after the
others ran the risk of no longer finding among the closely packed bodies
the spot to which he was entitled. I have seen many a comrade who, after
numerous insults, was forced to lie down on the thin fringe of flattened
straw along the sleepers' feet.

Well! in spite of the promiscuity which this detail enables one to imagine, it was interesting to see how the French found a way to preserve
their independence. You should have seen them during the day, each
had his own little occupation. Whether he cast aluminum rings or
carved a chess set, he did it all alone; to eat his soup, he would invariably
ferret out a stool; he had his frying pan made from half a canteen, and
in order to brown his herring he waited his turn at the stove. The insufficient space we had was utilized ingeniously so as to maintain the greatest possible discretion among us.

By contrast, the Russians did not even use all the space which was allocated to them. Spontaneously, they lived in an agglomerated state. They formed only one troop, a real "school." I can still see them, all gathered in a pack around the stove, endlessly telling each other stories (when I would ask them what they were doing: "*Onne razskazivaïette,** he is telling a story!" they would answer me), or singing in a chorus with a sweetness, a tenderness, and a harmony which was inimitable. Some would be sitting on stools, others would be standing behind them, others above them straddling saddle holders (we were quartered in a stable). And this staggering of levels was but the perceptible image of the mutual and quite natural meshing of their souls.

They had arguments among themselves which were perhaps more frequent and longlasting than ours. When one broke out, we could count on it to last the entire day. But right away one could feel an incredible lack of seriousness about it. It would flare like a fire close to the ground, but one which would never consume anything more than twigs. These were not individualities challenging each other, scrapping, looking for each other's weakness, or throwing each other on the ground. Nothing malicious, nothing deadly. In advance, we were sure that there would be no victims. All one had to do was to hear them chirping with their high-pitched voices, like those of a nestful of birds. They made fun of each other, and from time to time a tender laughter would shake the whole gathering. Above all, they had no desire to finish. Their disagreement among themselves was like the button passed and hidden in the hand and which goes around among all without anyone ever quite knowing where it is. Actually, it belonged to all of them at the same time, and that is the main reason why none of them would give in: the others would at once have considered him a robber.

Theirs are astonishingly little-retrenched souls. Nothing is easier for them than to dwell in each other. One must always remember Dostoevsky. How many of his characters merely have the "corner" of a bedroom sub-rented in someone else's home by way of dwelling? And there they live behind a curtain panel which is a marvelous symbol of what little separates their individuality from that of their neighbor. They exist, on the psychological level also, in a parasitical state; looking closely, one would find on each of them the dwelling of a least another.[2]

They are beings without a shell; they are gifted neither for defense and extremes, nor for attack and pretension. Among them the individual has no weight; his insufficient density forces him to fear shocks, prevents him from standing up. He asserts himself only through tenderness, complaint, cleverness, or betrayal. Surely, he does not lack per-

---

*As transcribed from Russian by Rivière.

sonality; but all its expressions are devious; to shake hands, beseech, cry, love, steal, deceive, flee: such are the ways by which it reveals itself. In order for it to develop fully, it must above all not encounter anyone; it blossoms only in a round-about way.

I do not know anything more admirable, more moving than Russian war songs. They are full of a timorous heroism. The fine Cossack, in all his accoutrements, goes off to war; he brandishes a lance; one hears his little horse trotting cheerfully. He is going to destroy everything, raze everything. The Turk will undergo cruel moments. But at least don't let the rascal get the idea of being too strong! The bold warrior would soon turn around; in the very cadence of victory, sketched as it were in reverse, there would appear, by the simplest of conversions, the cadence of flight.

I often walked alone along the side of our barracks: a Russian had taken the same habit and we would cross each other's path fifteen or twenty times in a row each day; he was a tall fellow who appeared to be quite healthy and robust; but I recall the way he would look at me in passing; I find his eyes in my memory, eyes which were so large, beautiful, loving, frightened, false: they hardly looked at me, they wished to win me over, they looked for the little door to my soul. But had I waved my arms, uttered and cry, right away they would have become elusive: I would have never seen them again.

So much timidity forbade the Russian all desire, all will to have individual freedom. It is not with his tender and flinching heart that he could wish for freedom and the right to do all he might wish. Nothing could be stranger to this sensitive and weak being than our hard ideal of independence and labor.

Nothing could be more odious to him. The Russian is in principle, if one may say so, and by his nature, against liberalism. One must understand the deep meaning of his hate for the Englishman. This man who is calm and strong, standing firm, well equipped, armed with his "habeas corpus" as if with a kind of waterproof, and who thinks first about doing business and about establishing himself well in this world; this man who is straight, plain, limited, peaceful, and pitiless, this great producer of wealth—the Russian holds it against him for being his most exact antithesis.

He execrates his unconstrained manners and his comfort as well as the way he is self-sufficient. He cannot bear a being who can stand up all alone, who comes and goes, who walks without ever thinking of others except in order to respect them. He discovers in him a horrible selfishness; his entrails stir against so much assurance and isolation.

No, indeed, he will never fall in love with as short and as fierce an ideal as liberalism. What use would his timid virtues find in it? How would he adapt his communicative and babbling soul to it?

Thus he does not find himself to be distinct and aggressive. He has no desire to make money and to establish himself. He needs no law to protect his initiative, and first of all, for the very good reason that he has no initiative.

On the contrary, he first needs to get recognized and his natural state sanctioned, which is a combination of his soul with others, an obscure brotherhood, a mysterious propensity to agglomerate. In Russia, there is no push by the individual as such, but a direct push by the masses. It is they which seek political autonomy. One should not expect to see this attained except by colonies of souls of the kind described earlier.[3]

Once free, the Russians could have only one idea: give birth to their internal socialism, bring about the soviet which they already formed within their hearts and souls. At bottom, Tsarism bothered them only to the extent that it wanted to force them into a general unity which went beyond their spontaneous power to aggregate. The violence which we pitied them for having to undergo, police brutality, illegal arrests, Siberia, all that they did not feel. Whoever knew their profound nature should have been able to foresee that the disappearance of Tsarist constraint could be greeted by them only as the means of at last organizing legally as they had been for a long time in fact, that is to say, in groups, in societies, in *soviets.*

Bolshevism may not be a viable regime; it is improbable that Russia should keep it definitively. But she will be able to replace it only by calling on foreigners, for it is quite evidently the most natural regime, the closest to its essence, she has ever known. It is the immediate product of its aspirations; in order to reach it, its wishes almost had no distance to cover; [the country] fell into it at the first step it tried to take all by itself.

One will see in Mr. Antonelli's so very interesting book on *Bolshevik Russia*, from which I quoted a passage earlier, how Lenin and Trotsky went about establishing their regime.[4] Actually, they did not really have to impose it; they merely followed psychology. Everywhere they foresaw and anticipated the essential desires of the masses. Differing from all the parties which had preceded them in power, they knew how to unravel the truly profound and primitive tendency of the Russian spirit, and their entire program was aimed at satisfying it. They were the first to understand that the Russian sought, yearned with all his instinct only for collective life, and that he dreamed of freedom only for the group to which he belonged.

The Bolsheviks have succeeded in transforming socialism exactly to the extent necessary so that it might become the most spontaneous and pleasant exercise the Russian people could wish of its psychological functions. Indeed:

> Breaking totally with Western methods with which the liberals or social-democrats were striving to veneer the old Slavic base during the first part of the Revolution, the Bolsheviks never conceived of power as a layer of authority spreading from the source to the people, so that the master of the source should always be the master of the dissemination of authority. On the contrary, they let authority emanate directly from the social mass without any sense of the unity of power or of the personality of the state. The legal anthropomorphism which created the state, the "legal being," the "moral person" which is merely a peculiar aspect of our Western philosophy which regards the individual as the purpose and center of law, is totally unknown to bolshevism. Thus one witnesses a confused and luxuriant flowering of authority, a strange overlapping, surprising apparent contradictions, which give us Westerners, with our geometrical soul, the impression of a complete hodge-podge, but which allows the Slavic soul to evolve quite freely through the midst of these contradictions and superpositions. Thus one will be able to see a "local" soviet—that of Moscow—decree the "nationalization" of the textile industry; sometimes it will even be a mere neighborhood—that of the Polustrovo—which will decree the "nationalization" of all buildings. One will see, in the same city, quite different authorities coexisting without being in violent opposition or real incoherence with each other. In Moscow, for example, anarchists will establish an authority completely distinct from that of the Bolsheviks, requisition buildings, and install services in them. Disorder is not increased: the black flag merely takes place of the red flag on the requisitioned premises.[5]

Bolshevism is the hardly organized, hardly systematized blooming of Russian instincts. What deceives us and leads us to believe that it is an adventitious and arbitrary regime, imposed by force on a recalcitrant mass, is the tyranny which it exerts on individuals. But we must realize that Russians have no way of perceiving this tyranny; it offends and goes against only their ideally weak inclinations, whereas it flatters and favors very powerful ones; and first of all, the need for collective command. The Russian cannot imagine anything more beautiful than being able to discuss, decree, domineer, but always by means of and through the intermediary of the group to which he adheres. He does not care if he is lectured to or even roughed up as an individual, he will readily accept the whip, as long as he is able as a member of some "council" to express his authority, prescribe regulations, dictate laws.

Again the *soviet* gives him all the satisfactions which he could ever have dreamt of: it is first of all a place where one is with several others, where one can chat and complain together: where without fear henceforth of being disturbed by the police one can give oneself up to the endless *razgavori*[6] mentioned by M. Antonelli.[7] Then it is a means of prescribing duties and responsibilities to individuals, to remind them, half scolding and half supplicating, of humility, charity, misery, of destroying this monstrous product of freedom which is wealth, to take Draconian measures against the selfish initiative of the industrialist or the merchant, to reduce anything that rises above the level of the Gospel by means of *prikasi*.[8] With this pettiness and his holiness, the Russian is wholly in the *soviet*. It is for him the ideal milieu, the only one in which he can really prosper and bear fruit. I would almost say that his real existence begins at the moment when his individual being thus comes to lose itself, or rather to find itself again in the social being, and that he receives the positive sign only when he integrates himself in this entity.

This is a fact whose importance must be fully understood for the future of the world. Until now, socialism has been something to be conceived, studied, or even applied. It existed in books and there were men of good will who with great effort were striving to make some of it occur in life. But the trouble they took was so great, the resistance they had to overcome was so strong and the results they attained so meager, that one might wonder in good faith whether their doctrine was anything more than a generous utopia, whether it could really be implemented.

Thanks to the Russians, a new era is beginning for socialism which is certainly not practical, not a realization, but—at the same time, something much more and much less—a reality. Socialists are being born, full-fledged socialists, before ever knowing of the doctrine, and who adopt it only because of its affinities with their temperament. People are being born who are setting out to live—well or badly? in happiness or wretchedness? the question remains open—anyway, to live socially.

Without having to force itself, a people is depriving itself of the desire to be free; at the very moment when the downfall of its "tyrant" gives it opportunity [to choose freedom], it prefers something else. It boldly and in one sweep leaps over the liberal phase of political evolution, which could have been regarded as unfeasible, and it goes back to offer its hands obediently to a new despot, the social despot. Or rather, it itself becomes this despot; it shows him to us in flesh and blood for the first time; doubtless, not as concentrated nor as "grouped" as theoretical descriptions lead us to expect, still in his natural state already endowed with life and breath: "The parts are good," we could say: each *soviet* already represents, in a sufficiently concrete fashion, this "direct authority of the social mass" which is an absolutely new phenomenon and the very possibility of which was until now subject to question. One must look things straight in the face: even if it is true that the Russian people are now undergoing hideous misery, even if they regret being Bolsheviks, a fact remains: they are Bolsheviks and through them, on one point of the globe, socialist existence has begun.

NOTES

1   This is the second part of "Décadence de la liberté," inspired by a depressing international situation (*N. R. F.*, XIII, September 1919, 498-522). Ten months after the Armistice which stopped the bloodiest war in history, fought by the Allies for right and freedom, Rivière felt that there was after all little demand for freedom. It appeared to him that by opting for communism, the Russians were in effect renouncing freedom.

2   In the Russian language itself, it constantly occurs that extra and adventitious letters come and become a part of words without its always being possible to explain this by the needs of euphony. That is what grammarians call *epenthesis* (see Reiff's Grammar). Similarly, almost every verb has several others which live off it, are nurtured by its forms, and add to it. Each action is expressed not by one single verb which would be conjugated so as to correspond to all its aspects, but by a group of verbs, both akin to and distinct from it, which take each other's place as it becomes necessary to face its different modalities. [J.R.]

3   "For him (i.e., the bolshevik) the individual is nothing; the soul, the idea, the 'Douch' [the spirit] is everything: the foundation of social life is not juridical but emotional." Etienne Antonelli: *La Russie bolchéviste*, p. 210, Bernard Grasset. [J.R.]

4   See especially chapter III: "The Bolsheviks and the People," p.69. [J.R.]

5   See *La Russie bolchéviste,* p.213-14 [J.R.]

6   Conversations, délibérations [J.R.]

7   See *La Russie bolchéviste,* p.72 [J.R.]

8   Orders, decrees (J.R.'s translation).

An Unpublished Version of
"Decadence of Freedom"*

Immediately, I add that I do not believe at all in the future of bolshevism as such. The very reasons which explain its importance seem likely to prevent its propagation—at least in its literal form—beyond the borders of the Slavic world. Its deep relationship with the Slavic soul, if it gives it spontaneity, paralyzes it in the same proportion: as it draws life from it, it also draws death.

Nothing is less fertile indeed than the Russian spirit, at least as far as practical things are concerned. It seems destined to succeed at nothing. This is a trait which I do not claim to have noticed first—anymore than those I recorded earlier—but on the contrary the evidence of it strikes everybody. [The Russian's] tendency to be attracted by the absolute, as writes M. Antonelli, "pushes him straight toward the ideal without taking into account the possible, the relative, the realizable" (p.71). In the behavior of bolshevik leaders, next to an undeniable political adaptability which M. Antonelli brings to light very well, there is rigidity, a tension, a monotony in their objectives, an almost fanatically direct approach to the absolute which ultimately is its principal characteristic. These people are possessed by a mysticism which is at least as strong as the rational mysticism of our revolutionary ancestors. They take as little account as they can of the moral as well as of the material obstacles which separate them from their dream. They do not make the smallest gesture in order to surmount them: they simply deny their existence, they suppress them mentally.

Rather—for it is perhaps necessary anyway to distinguish here between leaders such as Lenin and Trotsky, who have been made more realistic by the Western education which they have received, and the very mass of the Russian people which they would like to organize—there is in this mass a profound ignorance and even a profound disregard for the "means" which forever condemn all these ideals to wither on the vine. The mass imagines, conceives, wants: and from this point on everything appears done; nothing concerns it any longer; everyone returns home, no intervention is necessary any longer; life must at once take the course which has been presented to it.

We were able to see this psychology operating at the time of the peace [negotiations]. As long as the great principle of peace without indemni-

---

*This is an unpublished draft which Rivière probably intended to develop as a continuation of his article by the same title or in the context of a book.

ty or annexation had been proclaimed, all that remained to be done was to take the train and return home, "damoi." Reality was to follow automatically. It was not necessary for one to be present. The passage from the ideal to reality was to take place exactly as the passage from principle to consequences, deductively. All that was necessary was for the idea to be just, holy. How could man have another role, another duty, but to find it?

In spite of the leaders' efforts, I am convinced that it is in this fashion that the bolshevist program was applied in Russia. The socialization [sic: nationalization] of all property was proclaimed. Who could challenge the perfect beauty of this measure? Is it not the purest substance of the Gospel? Therefore, all is well. By this decree alone, the golden age begins. One needs no longer to stir, not even one's little finger. All one needs to do is to wait.

Doubtless—I too am convinced of it—there have been partial and textual implementations of the principles. From time to time a group would requisition an apartment building, expel its occupants, and move in. I have been told that one day in Moscow, Red Guards had come out of a car in front of a teahouse, had taken all the women who were inside, and purely and simply had "nationalized them." Even if the anecdote is [farfetched], it describes quite well the kind of implementation which one can expect from the Russians in the area of socialism: no follow-through, no logic, no unity; and at the same time vigorously literal. They have absolutely no knowledge of the resistance of matter. The truth is they have not even realized that their principle had not yet begun to live; it is quite naturally that they have begun to apply it in a given case; they have not realized that they were dealing with an exception; they believed they were merely pursuing a work already accomplished; unbeknown to them, their action prolonged quite naturally that which had remained for them only a thought.

In other words, the Russian mind does not perceive intermediary stages. It conceives and does. But between the first and the second stage the transition is abrupt. It lacks the ability to break down a principle into detailed stages which take reality into account, which establish contact with reality, which strive to divide it and assimilate it, to overcome it; it does not even know how to insinuate itself between them.

This socialism is applied by the bolshevists but in a form which is, so-to-speak, negative. Soviets are indeed true socialist organs, but for the time being they function only destructively. All that can be negated, they negate.

Everything that is not social and does not belong to the masses or does not benefit them they eliminate. But it seems to me that they are

162

not even capable of transferring the benefit to them. They seem incapable of finding the means by which to transfer it from society to the individual. As I was saying earlier, deep down they are working but toward the establishment of an even level everywhere, a level of misery (wretchedness).

In my mind this is not only a criticism. The modern world would be in great need of "pauperization." Its wealth chokes it and soils it to such a point that it does not even notice it, which is the worst part. But because I endorse it to a certain extent from a Christian point of view, I cannot help seeing from a critical point of view that Bolshevism in its Russian form cannot succeed. It is absurd to assume that the entire world is going to give up purely and simply and without compensation all the material advantages which progress has given to it and the means, however cruel, however pitiless, by which they were obtained.

Bolshevism has no chance of converting a civilization such as ours or that of England, and the threat to individual existence and freedom which it represents will remain without danger if it were not taken up in a more precise, in a more "modern", more practical and more organic form by Germany. The Russians will have given concrete examples of socialist existence. But it is an innovation which will remain purely static. The prodigious dynamism of the Germans may be capable of transforming this existence into a socialist one whose effects it is hardly possible to evaluate at this time.

Russian Ballets at the Opera:
*La Boutique fantasque, The Three-Cornered Hat,
The Song of the Nightingale*[1]
by Jacques Rivière

It has already been a very long time since M. de Diaghilev's troupe
left Russia; even before 1914, it lost all firm ties with its country of origin and had begun to wander through the world. It seems, however, that
the war and the Russian Revolution have increased the separation from
fatherland and definitively severed it from its basis.

"By the hurricane, thrown in an air without birds."[2]

M. de Diaghilev did not resign himself in a cowardly way to his solitude; on the contrary, he has tried to find about him collaborators and
aides; he has established ties with artists in the countries he visited; as
skillfully as possible he has assimilated the substance he could gather
abroad. In his last creations especially, the French element, the Spanish,
and even the Italian have gained considerable importance.

It is therefore mostly cross-bred works that we are invited to judge today. This aspect gives them quite a special interest, but it may also
explain why none of these works succeeds in giving us a perfectly pure
and homogeneous impression and that mixed with the pleasure they
provide us there is a certain hesitation of the mind and a rather painful
pang of the senses. Our attention is satisfied without previous agreement, without a sufficient intimacy among those who solicit it: consequently it receives only a partial and as if fragmented satisfaction.
Here we are far indeed from those complete and harmonious successes
called *Prince Igor, Petrushka, Le Sacre du Printemps.* We must say
it frankly: this is no longer the time when all our senses, our heart itself,
found at once in Russian ballets a refreshing and delicious potion. Our
curiosity alone still keeps us attached to it, and it is only because we feel
this caress within us that we can henceforth expect pleasure.

Nijinski's disappearance reveals itself as being of such serious consequence that even the 1914 season could not yet make us foresee.
Massine's ingenuity as dancer and as choreographer merely underscores
Nijinski's real genius. The latter's absence is as it were visible; one feels
him removed, as it were, from all the gestures and all the movements
which are offered to us. It is especially today when he is no longer here to
radiate it that one can realize the extraordinary power of radiance this
man had. When he dances, Massine can have a charming silhouette: but
nothing ever emanates from it, it does not separate itself from him; it

164

does not propagate; it remains strict, deft and thin. With Karsavina he never succeeds in forming that heady couple to which Nijinski knew how to give birth so well. He does not have, like Nijinski, the art of hatching this woman, of making her blossom. The young Bacchus is no longer here, through whom frenzy ecstasy, and the kiss formerly flowed brimming full.

Not only that, but Massine's choreographic invention has nothing spontaneous about it; it more or less painfully follows in the steps traced by Nijinski. Everything imagined by Massine in the way of step and gesticulation (outside of what he borrows textually from popular dance) has its evident source in the *Sacre du Printemps*: these stampings, this way of outlining the sky with one arm above the head, these broken attitudes, all this comes directly and without real transposition from the *Sacre*. But the closer imitation is, the deeper the abyss which separates the copy from the original, for one notices more that it lacks all the necessity that filled it. There was indeed a reason for the awkward and spasmodic choreography of Nijinski's ballet: it was the subject itself, the panic atmosphere the authors had intended to create; it was the heaviness of Spring, it was the fixity of prehistoric life which overburdened, forced, and thus reduced movements. In the ballets directed by Massine, one looks in vain for a justification of the skimpy gait of the dance, for its perpetual cramp. *The Song of the Nightingale* itself, in spite of the stifling and contracted elements which Stravinsky's music introduces into it, does not however imply a sufficient horror for us to be able to explain so many contortions, such complicated gymnastics, such a great poverty of grace and élan.

Massine was a talented dancer; contrary to appearances, fate has played a very bad trick on him by suddenly calling on him to take Nijinski's place; puff himself up as he might, for him to occupy it entirely he had to have something else besides elegance and good will.

With these reservations, whose seriousness I do not hide, one must recognize nonetheless that none of this year's three new shows is boring, and that one finds even very pleasant parts. I am not wild over the décor which André Dérain has painted for the *Boutique fantasque*.[3] Primitivism in it is somewhat contrived; the big figures which decorate the curtain are so awkwardly done that one feels they really gave the author too much trouble. Furthermore, the décor is a little too vast for it to be great; too much air circulates through it; it does not sufficiently imprison the dancers, it does not rouse them enough.

As far as costumes are concerned, they lack exaggeration. Their bad taste is too stingy. The characters attain the grotesque only through little accents applied from the outside; the ridiculous does not erupt from their vitals; it is insufficiently artesian.

But the work is amusing, full of dash, aplomb, and a fine impertinence. At first a little too close to pantomime or even comedy, it becomes progressively animated, and toward the end we find several of those beautiful and structured tumults, those graceful castles of gestures which formerly held us in rapture.

If M. de Falla's music were less servilely inspired by Spanish folklore and above all if it had a little more harmonic distinction, *The Three-Cornered Hat*[4] would be the masterpiece of the season. After a dreadful and inexplicable railroad poster with which for some mysterious reason Picasso thought it necessary to afflict our eyes for a moment, the curtain rises on a truly delightful décor, which one soon discovers was calculated with admirable care to form the most diverse harmonies with the dark elegance of the costumes. One has a feeling here of all that Picasso would be capable of if only he could lose this prospector's mania which always leads him by preference on paths where he is assured no one will follow him and which makes him place the acme of art in the continual obliteration of his own tracks. Here for once he is without any other desire but to please, and he succeeds at once with a good fortune which many will envy. Yet I imagine that this success must leave him not without remorse, and that he is already thinking of ways to make us forget it. Too bad! But let us think only of our pleasure, which is great.

I am not sufficiently competent to distinguish what the choreography of *The Three-Cornered Hat* owes to popular Spanish dance. If I were told that it had been entirely transposed from it, I would not be excessively astonished. But why should I complain about it, since it is the liveliest, the most spontaneous, the merriest that Massine has been able to manage? The step he dances himself alone gives us at times as it were a hallucinatory vision of Nijinski: it is the greatest praise one can make about it.

As a whole, *The Song of the Nightingale*[5] is without any doubt at the same time the least successful and the richest of the three new ballets. It is an arduous, pretentious, magnificent work, crammed with intelligence and full of rarity. It is as if Matisse had digested China with his acid brain and had found it reduced to three or four fundamental colors with which right away he boldly plastered flat his entire décor. At first sight, its effect is striking: one finds it a little easier after some thought. One does not tire of it, however, as rapidly as the mind would wish. This is because the extreme tonal simplicity on which the costumes undertake a frank and suave commentary gives to the show as a whole a cohesion and a harmony which one cannot prevent oneself from feeling with satisfaction, especilly after having seen the *Boutique fantasque*. When the all-white Nightingale leads away the red she-monkey of death held prisoner by its collar, as studied as their steps and attitudes may be, the impression is strong, were it only because of the atrocious limpidity with which our eyes are filled.

Stravinsky is a prodigious musician. I do not feel an immediate rapport with some of the works which he composed during the war and which he let us hear at a recent Delgrange concert. But none diminishes the confidence I have in the author of *Petrushka* and of *Le Sacre du Printemps*, which remain the only two truly great works one has seen appear since *Pelléas*.

To tell the truth, at the first hearing of *The Song of the Nightingale* I again felt the malaise which I described in this same review in July 1914, at the time the work had first appeared in the form of an opera; again it has appeared too strangled, too slow, and too short at the same time, too constantly inspired by suicide. But I have heard it again, and without being able to completely rid myself of what annoyed me in it, I became more sensitive to the extraordinary quality of its detail.

I know of nothing more astonishing than Stravinsky's tranquility in the face of the somber birds which the cage of his mind lets out one by one. How is it that he is not afraid? Each in turn comes forward in the void of the orchestra, hops, turns, flutters its wings a little, sings an instant without echo, and perishes. There are gulfs of silence where strange vibrios turn. All of a sudden, everything is set in motion all together, like the paddle-wheels of a mill, like the thousand hammers of a factory: instruments which have not in the least been aligned in advance, start off as a group; they fall in together as they go along, as good comrades would. Then a sour, low melody travels alone for a moment on some kind of mysterious little feet under its belly. And again nothing: music reverts to the form of silence; the orchestra shows its inwards; sounds spread out and absorb us in the bottom of a monstrous vat where we will be subjected to a whole system of strung-out tortures.

One should not forget that the formidable freedom from which flow the taste and discretion enjoyed by young musicians today is owed to Stravinsky, to this frail Samson who with an easy blow and as if in deep sleep has pushed back all the wall of the temple of music.

NOTES

1   This essay appeared first in the *N.R.F.*, XIV (March 1920) 462-67 and was reprinted in *Nouvelles Etudes*, (Paris: Gallimard, 1947).

2   "Jeté par l'ouragan dans l'éther sans oiseaux," *Le Bateau ivre*, Arthur Rimbaud.

3   *La Boutique Fantasque*. Ballet in one act. Music by Giacomo Rossini, arranged and orchestrated by Ottorino Respighi. Choreography by Léonide Massine. Curtain, décor, and costumes by André Dérain. First performance: Alhambra Theatre, London, June 5, 1919 (Kochno, *Diaghilev*, 126).

4   *The Three-Cornered Hat*. Ballet in one act, by Martinez Sierra, after the tale by Pedro Antonio de Alarcon. Music by Manuel de Falla. Choreography by Léonide Massine. Curtain, décor, and costumes by Pablo Picasso. First performance: Alhambra Theatre, London, July 22,1919.

"In the spring of 1926, the sale of the curtain Picasso had painted for *Le Tricorne* saved the life of the Ballets Russes. Diaghilev had no funds either for company salaries or for the production of new works. With Picasso's consent, he sold through Paul Rosenberg, the art dealer, the central panel of the *Tricorne* curtain and the figure paintings in the décor for *Cuadro Flamenco*" (Kochno,*Diaghilev*,136).

5   Ballet in one act after the fairy tale by Hans Christian Andersen. Music by Igor Stravinsky. Choreography by Léonide Massine. Curtain, décor, and costumes by Henri Matisse. First performance: Théâtre National de l'Opéra, Paris, February 2, 1910 (Kochno, *Diaghilev*, 138).

The Ukrainian Chorus
under the Direction of Professor Kochitz
at the *Théâtre des Champs-Elysées*[1]

The hands of M. Kochitz! The soft home dough, so modestly perfumed, which they knead! The sweet peasant cake which they make for us!

This music is not absolutely first rate, these popular songs have quite evidently undergone arrangements not always inspired by genius....We are far from Mussorgsky. But the way all this "comes out," the murmurs, the puffs, the pauses, the humming, the quick and naïve outbursts, one thinks of a bee in the garden or of some marvelous accordion in the back of an enchanted izba!

Well! it will not be easy to replace the Russians, or even the Little Russians. So much childhood cannot be reinvented, and our voices will never be able to go so far beyond the word, beyond the thought, back to this pure, timid, confident bouquet!

NOTES

1 "Le Choeur Ukrainien," N.R.F., XVI (May 1921) 626-27.

On Dostoevsky and the Unfathomable[1]
by Jacques Rivière

Once a novelist has imagined a character, there are two quite different ways in which he can develop it: either he can insist on its complexity, or he can underscore its coherence; in this soul to which he is about to give birth, he may either wish to produce all darkness or he may want to eliminate it for the reader; in depicting this soul, either he will withhold its depths or he will explore them.

André Gide has quite appropriately defined elsewhere[2] the reasons for which Dostoevsky has met with so much incomprehension in France. One should, I believe, add to these the following: in his psychological inventions, he always follows the first of the above methods, whereas all our gifts have always inclined us [French] to practice only the second.

One can feel that the fact which struck Dostoevsky the most and to which he determined to remain faithful from one end of his work to the other is the cohabitation in each conscience of contradictory and irreducible instincts. He may be the first to have squarely and resolutely faced the absurdity of our sentiments such as they spontaneously combine within us, and in a movement of enthusiasm and love for human nature dared to embrace this absurdity as an ideal. He tries to reveal it in all his characters and even especially those for whom he has sympathy.

He would almost exaggerate the disorder he finds in his models; with his own hand he would break the threads which in spite of everything keep together the network of their aspirations; he would carry disorder and lack of coordination into the sequence of their feelings.

In any case, he is interested above all in their depths, and it is in suggesting these depths as unfathomable as possible that he puts his greatest care. As he breathes fictional life into his character (and this is the means he chooses to give him life), he concentrates on bringing out the insufficiency of the reasons through which one might be tempted to explain his determinations; he establishes a relationship every time between these determinations and an X which is the only basis he consents to give this soul. And far from pursuing the definition of this X, he constantly withdraws from us the means which we think we see as known values to enter into the equation.

On the contrary, when we [French] are faced with the complexity of a soul, as we try to describe it, we instinctively try to organize it. Even our description is an effort toward integration. Something within us which we are not able to control unleashes itself at once and shows us the inner connections of the model, the solidarity of its aspects. If need be, we lend a hand: we suppress a few divergent traits, we interpret a few obscure details in such a way as to constitute a psychological unity.

We are always reluctant in tracing the portrait of a character to leave something indefinite: "There was something indefinable in all of Monsieur de la Rochefoucauld," writes the Cardinal de Retz. Yes, but precisely, he expresses it so that the reader would not have to feel it.

Never, in the character created, does a wide open gap remain through which unforeseen inspirations could come to him. When we make him speak, never does anything give an inexplicable sound, never does anything give out a sound which is different for the mind and the imagination. We penetrate into the interstices of his character with our laboriously produced wax and we cement them. The perfect filling of its abysses is the ideal toward which we aim. And I imagine this is what bothers foreigners in Racine's Nero or even Stendhal's Julien. We never show the vertigo of the human soul.

*

It is Dostoevsky who was first to make me feel our insufficiency on this point. I was overwhelmed by this for a long time, and nothing in the world would have made me compare our novelists or our dramatists to the terrifying evocator of the unknown which I discovered in him.

And then, little by little, thoughts came to me which are directed not against Dostoevsky's work but against the excellence, or at least against the supremacy, of his method.

First this thought: an abyss is nothing as long as we do not go down into it. I am far from claiming that what I am going to say about this is so in Dostoevsky's novels; but after all, an abyss can very well be faked. One can very well capture and direct our attention toward the far reaches of a soul without, however, their losing their hypothetical nature. The fact that a character acts in an inexplicable fashion does not necessarily imply that there are in him depths which nothing will ever enable us to reach: such a character could also have been inspired by mere inconsistency, which is superficial and definable.

After all, the explanation of a human being does not *a priori* involve any more arrangement and artifice than does insistence on its mystery. It is only a matter of not going wrong, of not going against life. Nothing will ever make me believe that with enough intuition it is impossible to give a character both depth and consistency.

We French should beware of our natural tendency to simplify, to reduce things to a given denominator. But if we merely guard ourselves

171

against this tendency and never let it dominate the complexity of reality, it can enable us to see connections which are also real and which are also a part of psychological nature.

For in short, as unusual as the human being may be, as long as he is not insane, and perhaps even when he is, he never escapes certain principles of a fundamental logic. There is a connection between one of his actions and the next; he may constantly act against reason and yet be obeying a certain idea. Let us use more vague terms: he may be following a certain disposition, a certain bent of his brain which models his entire spiritual life. And even when he contradicts himself, who can assert, as long as he has analyzed him, that his contradiction is anything other than the rafraction, through events, of a simple tendency?

Rather than lead the mind astray toward a psychological infinity, one can very well conceive that task of the novelist as bringing it back by the mere continuity of his descriptions toward this secret but concrete and knowable event. The work of his reason can very well help him in his representation of life. While drawing him, he can look for an individual's principles without necessarily falling into abstraction and schematization. His patience, his instinctive feeling for detecting that which resists clarification will be of the highest importance. But if he has this gift at the same time as what I would call the faculty of adhering to intuition, he will be able to produce a work which will surpass, even in depth, all that Dostoevsky's adventurous genius could create. For in psychology, I must be permitted to say it again, true depths are those which are explored.

NOTES

1   "De Dostoievski et de l'insondable." *N.R.F.*, XVIII (February 1922) 175-78. Another translation of this essay appeared under the title "On Dostoevsky and the Creation of Character" in *The Ideal Reader: Selected Essays by Jacques Rivière*, edited, translated and introduced by Blanche A. Price, with a preface by Henri Peyre (New York: Meridian Books, 1960). The present translation owes to it several felicitous turns of phrase.

Originally, in his rough draft, Rivière had entitled his article "A Little Defense of French Psychology Against Dostoevsky." After having evoked the time when he was profoundly influenced by the Russian writer, both esthetically and spiritually, Rivière explains that he "simply feels the need to react against the writer and especially against his psychological method or rather against those who would present it as the only one capable of leading one to extreme depth." Later, he expresses his belief that there is a certain psychological coherence in all human beings: "It is evident that there is an apparent incoherence in our actions, a superficial scattering of our minds, [...]. But there is also logic of the personality which it may be the business of psychology to find and bring out."

2   André Gide, *Dostoievski* (Paris: Plon, 1929)

CONCLUSION

The evolution of Rivière's thought and attitude toward the Russians and his opinion of their culture modified his insights into the future development of communism in the Soviet Union. It can also be considered as being a typical and enlightening experience by an intellectual of good will.

Toward the end of his captivity, after three years of close daily contact with the Russians and intense study of their language, Rivière experienced disillusionment both with the Russian people and their civilization. Political changes occurring in Russia at the time were under intense discussion among prisoners of war as everywhere else in the Western World. Specifically, it was the advent of socialism which inspired Rivière's reassessment of Russian civilization as a whole and his disillusionment with it.

The Bolshevik revolution first came to Rivière as a surprise. It forced him to conclude that he had not "penetrated to the depths of the Russian soul, the most difficult, the most secret, the most disappointing, I think," he wrote, "that in its essence it remains forever inaccessible." Nonetheless, he attempted to explain how communism could become established in Russia by advancing a number of theories about the mentality of the Russian people. "The Russian is in principle, if one may say so, and by his nature, against liberalism." Certainly, in this case he was basing his views on his knowledge of history rather than on any specific aspect of Russian mentality. Similarly, he tried to explain the Russians' "acceptance" of centralized planning by their alleged lack of initiative. He also felt that Russians did not feel the tyranny of communism because of the insufficient development of individualism within their culture. Consequently, he imagined the the Russian masses might willingly accept the Soviet system as a means of channeling authority, in collective and egalitarian fashion, from the grass-roots level to the top. In this, Rivière proved to be utterly wrong. It was perhaps too early to determine that in the Soviet Union all authority is centralized at the top whence it flows down to the masses; the latter have virtually no means of modifying either the direction of the flow of power nor its nature as it affects all aspects of life.

Whereas his conjectures on the Russians' propensity for collectivism are very debatable, other notions Rivière advanced have, in time, been corroborated. He did see that communist revolutionary mysticism would obfuscate objectivity and inspire disregard for the means employed in attaining idealistic goals and that consequently revolutionary action and idealism are often in opposition to each other. Rivière correctly saw that in Russia socialism was being applied negatively against an order and an *ethos* so as "to establish equality [or rather] an equal level of misery."

When he wrote that Lenin and Trotsky "merely anticipated essential desires of the masses" and that they knew "how to unravel the truly profound and primitive tendency of the Russian spirit and that their entire program was aimed at satisfying it," he was simply not taking mass psychology into account. As some nineteenth century sociologists have explained, the level of thought in a mass is inferior to that of most individuals within it. During the Russian Revolution, as during the French, leaders unleashed not the most profound feeling among their people but the most paltry, vicious envy and used this instinctively hidden feeling as a motor of action.

Rivière felt that "just as a very clear demarcation between individuals develops and enhances the feeling of ownership, so does communal life weaken it." He was correct, however, at least until now, to say that Bolshevism in its Russian form cannot succeed in France or England because "[Westerners] exist as individuals before they exist as members of social groups. One could say the opposite of the Russians."

Communism, he thought, would represent no danger for Western civilization unless adopted by Germany, which he felt might be tempted by it and would have the energy and organizational ability to spread it beyond the Slavic world. A quarter of a century later, in spite of the Germans, communism had engulfed by force all of the Slavic world and today controls to various degrees numerous underdeveloped countries as well. Although Germany as a whole remains an essential prize, both for the strengthening of the Soviet Union and the spread of communism, again, as have so many other observers, Rivière attributed far too great an importance to alleged Russian backwardness and simply failed to realize that as soon as it was established in Russia, communism would be used as a tool of the very old, tenacious, and ambitious Russian imperialism. Indeed, for many years, like most Westerners, Rivière failed to realize the great ethnic diversity of the Russian Empire and of the Soviet Union. In the confusion and mêlée following the break-up of the Tsarist empire, ethnic groups such as the Estonians, Latvians and Lithuanians (who shared neither Russian mentality nor communist ideology) won their independence, while the Ukrainians, the largest ethnic minority, fought unsuccessfully for their freedom. Rivière sensed correctly, however, that the Russians would not use their power to advance "worthy goals," such as freedom. Furthermore, he felt it "improbable that Russia would keep [the communist system] indefinitely." Only with the help of foreigners, he thought, would she be able to rid herself of this system. Indeed, so far there has been no successful attempt in the Soviet Union to overthrow communism from within. In satellite countries Solidarity failed so far for lack of external help. In his deep disappointment, Rivière stated that communism was "the most natural regime, the closest to its essence [Russia] has ever known." The greatest shortcoming in his assessment of Russian communism remains, however, his misunderstanding of the extraordinary power of the communist apparatus.

In addition to the repressive power of security organs and other bureaucratic structures, the complex of inferiority felt by the Russians vis-à-vis the Western world has been cleverly used by Soviet authorities. Since the Second World War students of the Soviet Union such as George K. Kennan have understood this complex well, although they have not shown the correlation between it and the still common historical anti-Slavic attitude of the West. "To show the West!" is perhaps one of the greatest motivating forces of the Russians and one point on which they are able to rally the support of other Slavic peoples. On balance, Rivière's reappraisal of Russian attitudes and his insights into the momentous changes occurring in Russia remain useful. Where he was wrong, he has hardly been corrected; where he was right, he has not been heeded.

*

Rivière's study of Russian culture and mentality is not unique as an intellectual experience and it continues to have significance. In fact, it remains typical of the way in which intellectuals approach the study of a foreign culture and of their overall experience with it.

Numerous intellectuals have been attracted by Russian culture because it has been isolated from the West and it consequently has considerable exotic appeal. Before and since the Russian Revolution, numerous students of Russian culture have, like Rivière, experienced disillusionment after enthusiasm. In fact, the sequence of enthusiasm-disenchantment is a phenomenon which deserves further study. Clearly, even in Rivière's case, communism, although a determining factor, was not the only cause of his disenchantment. In the normal course of study of a foreign civilization, the initial contact is through literature, art, and music, which are the highest and most beautiful manifestations of a people's activities, its "high culture." They inspire a desire for more contacts, and as these increase, their quality declines. Quite naturally, the average cultural level of a people or a country is lower than that of its high culture. Unless well understood, this differential inevitably causes disappointment in the admirer of the foreign country. This, no doubt, happened to Rivière as it happens in the case of all students of foreign cultures unless the individual loses his identity to embrace the foreign one.

Literature and the arts in general are representative expressions of only a part of a people's activity and of its soul. Hence, they cannot be the only basis by which to study an entire people without risk of error or disappointment. In Rivière's case, disenchantment was precipitated and exacerbated by the establishment of communism in Russia because the nature of this regime had special implications and significance for him as an artist and a patriot. At once, he realized that in a communist system the condition of the artist would be radically changed. To him, creative activity was the result of individual effort and could be carried out only in a climate of freedom. Yet he knew that freedom would be thwarted by collectivism. Moreover, as a Frenchman he sensed that the culture to be generated by communism in Russia, or elsewhere, would be antithetical to the basically aristocratic culture of France even in its contemporary form modified by bourgeois mentality.

On both these grounds, Rivière's insights proved to be correct: the spiritual condition of the artist has been anything but favorable to the creative process, and the influence of communism on art and literature in general has been antithetical to the French taste and tradition still cherished by men of his generation.

Given his grave reservations and torment regarding the horrible exploitation of workers during the industrialization of the West, Rivière, as have so many others since, was fascinated by the socialist ideal of justice. He remained on the horns of a dilemma, for he could accept neither the loss of freedom nor could he tolerate the social injustices inherent to the capitalist system.

SELECTIVE BIBLIOGRAPHY

I.   Works by Jacques Rivière.

Etudes. Paris: Editions de la N.R.F., 1911. Reprinted with a foreword in 1924.

L'Allemand, Souvenirs et Réflexions d'un prisonnier de guerre. Paris: Gallimard, 1918. Reprinted with a foreword in 1924.

Aimée. Paris: Gallimard, 1922.

Marcel Proust. Monaco: Imprimerie de Monaco, 1924.

A la Trace de Dieu, avec une préface de Paul Claudel. Paris: Gallimard, 1925.

Quelques Progrès dans l'étude du coeur humain (Freud et Proust). Paris: Librairie de France, 1926.

Correspondance 1907-1914 (J. Rivière et P. Claudel). Paris: Plon, 1926.

Correspondance 1905-1914 (J. Rivière et Alain- Fournier), 4 vols. Paris: Gallimard, 1926-1928. Nouvelle édition, revue et augmentée, 2 vols., 1948.

De la Sincérité envers soi-même (and other essays), introduction by Isabelle Rivière. Paris: Aux Horizons de France, 1927. Reprinted by Gallimard, 1943.

Le Français. Paris: Editions Claude Aveline, 1928.

Carnet de guerre, août-septembre, 1914 Paris: Editions de la Belle Page, 1929.

Pour et contre une Société des Nations (1917-1918). Cahiers de la Quinzaine, 14ème cahier de la 19ème série. Paris: Artisan du Livre, 1930.

Moralisme et Littérature (avec Ramon Fernandez). Paris: Corrêa, 1932.

Florence, a novel with an introduction by Isabelle Rivière. Paris: Corrêa, 1935.

Nouvelles Etudes. Paris: Gallimard, 1947.

The Ideal Reader: Selected Essays by Jacques Rivière. Edited, translated and introduced by Blanche A. Price, with a preface by Henri Peyre. New York: Meridian Books, 1960.

Carnets (1914-1917) Introduction and notes by Isabelle Rivière and Alain Rivière. Paris: Fayard, 1974.

Correspondance 1909-1925 (J. Rivière et Jean Schlumberger): Lyon: Centre d'Etudes Gidiennes, 1980.

II.   Studies on Jacques Rivière

Beaulieu, Paul. *Jacques Rivière*. Paris: La Colombe, Ed. du Vieux-Colombier, 1956.

Chaix, Joseph. *De Renan à Jacques Rivière: Dilettantisme et amoralisme*. Paris: Bloud et Gay, 1930.

Charlot, Pierre. *Jacques Rivière, une vie ardente et sincère*. Paris: Bloud et Gay, 1934.

Cook,Bradford: *Jacques Rivière: A Life of the Spirit.* Oxford: Basil Blackwell, 1958.

Coquoz, François-Marie. *L'Evolution religieuse de J. Rivière.* Fribourg: Editions Universitaires, 1963.

Naughton, Helen Thomas. *Jacques Rivière. The Development of a Man and a Creed.* The Hague and Paris: Mouton, 1966.

Price, Blanche. *Jacques Rivière and His Literary Critics.* Ann Arbor: Michigan, University Microfilms, No. 6686, 1953.

Raymond, Marcel. *Etudes sur Jacques Rivière.* Paris: Librairie José Corti, 1972.

Rivière, Isabelle: *Le Bouquet de roses rouges.* Paris: Corrêa, 1935.

--------. *Vie et Passion d'Alain Fournier.* Monaco: Jaspard, Polus and Cie, 1963.

Suffran, Michael. *Jacques Rivière ou la conversion à la clarté.* Paris: Wesmael-Charlier, 1967.

Turnell, Martin. *Jacques Rivière.* New Haven: Yale University Press, 1953.

INDEX

184

Socialism, 30, 31, 32, 105, 107, 125, 127, 130, 131, 132, 133, 134, 138, 157, 159, 162, 173, 174
Solidarity, 175
The Song of the Nightingale by I. Stravinsky, 164-167, 168
soviet, a, 157, 158, 160, 162; the Soviets, 31; the soviet government, 14; the soviet phenomenon, 154; the soviet system, 159, 173; the Soviet Union, 116, 141, 173, 174, 175; the Soviet World, 174
Le Spectre de la Rose by C. M. von Weber, 65, 67, 76, 81
Stendhal, 147, 171
The Stone Guest by Alexander S. Dargomyzhsky, 22
The Stormy Petrel by Maxim Gorki, 34
Strauss, Richard, 86, 93, 94
Stravinsky, Igor, 19, 23, 25, 31, 39, 42, 43, 45, 46, 58, 59, 60, 65-94, 141, 165, 167, 168
Suarès, André, 47
Sumarokov, Aleksandr P., 16
Symphonic Suites by P. I. Tchaikowsky, 22

Tartars, 11, 15
Tchaikovsky, Peter Ilyich, 22, 23, 25
Tcherepnin, Nicholas, 25, 95
Tête d'Or by Paul Claudel, 64, 85
Thamar by M. Balakirev, 77, 85
Théâtre des Arts, Le, 55, 57
Théâtre des Champs-Elysées, le, 48, 65, 67, 169
Théâtre du Châtelet, le, 67
Théâtre National de l'Opéra, see Paris Opera
The Thousand and One Nights, 42, 65
The Three-Cornered Hat (Le Tricorne) by Martinez Sierra and Manuel de Falla, 164, 166, 168
Tintoretto, 94
Tolstoi, Count Lev N., 12, 16, 19, 20, 31, 32, 101, 125, 151
Tretiakov, Pavel, 24
Tristan and Isolde by Richard Wagner, 87
Trotsky, Leon, 157, 161, 174
Troyat, Henri, 108
The Tsarist Empire, 116, 123, 174; tsarist regime, 140, 157
Tsushima Strait, 24
Tuileries, 134, 136
Turgeniev, Ivan S., 18-19, 20, 24, 37
Turkish Empire (Ottoman Empire), 11

Ukrainians, 141, 169, 174
Uniates, the, 124
United States of Europe, the, 104, 131

Valéry, Paul, 141
Vaudoyer, Jean-Louis, 67
Vereshchagin, Vasili, 24, 25
Veronese, Paolo, 94
Viardot, Louis, 18
Viazemsky, Prince Peter A., 17, 18
Vogüé, Eugène Marie Melchior, vicomte de, 11, 19, 20, 32, 47
Voltaire, 11, 16, 17
Vrubel, Mikhail A., 24

Wagner, Richard, 23, 35, 87
War and Peace by L. Tolstoi, 16
West, the 15, 66, 104, 123, 148, 175, 176; Western civilization, 11, 174; culture,
    144; democracies, 104, education, 126, 161; Europe, 12, 18, 30, 141; Euro-
    peans (Westerners), 11, 29, 32, 42, 43, 50, 66, 114, 115, 116, 118, 144, 158, 174;
    methods, 158; mind, 12; society, 133; world, 15
World War I, 12, 20, 30, 32, 33, 36, 45, 46, 100, 108
Wuthering Heights by Emily Brontë, 40

Zhukovsky, Vasily A., 18

EAST EUROPEAN MONOGRAPHS

The *East European Monographs* comprise scholarly books on the history and civilization of Eastern Europe. They are published under the editorship of Stephen Fischer-Galati, in the belief that these studies contribute substantially to the knowledge of the area and serve to stimulate scholarship and research.

1. *Political Ideas and the Enlightenment in the Romanian Principalities, 1750–1831.* By Vlad Georgescu. 1971.
2. *America, Italy and the Birth of Yugoslavia, 1917–1919.* By Dragan R. Zivjinovic. 1972.
3. *Jewish Nobles and Geniuses in Modern Hungary.* By William O. McCagg, Jr. 1972.
4. *Mixail Soloxov in Yugoslavia: Reception and Literary Impact.* By Robert F. Price. 1973.
5. *The Historical and Nationalist Thought of Nicolae Iorga.* By William O. Oldson. 1973.
6. *Guide to Polish Libraries and Archives.* By Richard C. Lewanski. 1974.
7. *Vienna Broadcasts to Slovakia, 1938–1939: A Case Study in Subversion.* By Henry Delfiner. 1974.
8. *The 1917 Revolution in Latvia.* By Andrew Ezergailis. 1974.
9. *The Ukraine in the United Nations Organization: A Study in Soviet Foreign Policy. 1944–1950.* By Konstantin Sawczuk. 1975.
10. *The Bosnian Church: A New Interpretation.* By John V. A. Fine, Jr., 1975.
11. *Intellectual and Social Developments in the Habsburg Empire from Maria Theresa to World War I.* Edited by Stanley B. Winters and Joseph Held. 1975.
12. *Ljudevit Gaj and the Illyrian Movement.* By Elinor Murray Despalatovic. 1975.
13. *Tolerance and Movements of Religious Dissent in Eastern Europe.* Edited by Bela K. Kiraly. 1975.
14. *The Parish Republic: Hlinka's Slovak People's Party, 1939–1945.* By Yeshayahu Jelinek. 1976.
15. *The Russian Annexation of Bessarabia, 1774–1828.* By George F. Jewsbury. 1976.
16. *Modern Hungarian Historiography.* By Steven Bela Vardy. 1976.
17. *Values and Community in Multi-National Yugoslavia.* By Gary K. Bertsch. 1976.
18. *The Greek Socialist Movement and the First World War: the Road to Unity.* By George B. Leon. 1976.
19. *The Radical Left in the Hungarian Revolution of 1848.* By Laszlo Deme. 1976.
20. *Hungary between Wilson and Lenin: The Hungarian Revolution of 1918–1919 and the Big Three.* By Peter Pastor. 1976.

21. *The Crises of France's East-Central European Diplomacy, 1933–1938.* By Anthony J. Komjathy. 1976.

22. *Polish Politics and National Reform, 1775–1788.* By Daniel Stone. 1976.

23. *The Habsburg Empire in World War I.* Edited by Robert A. Kann, Bela K. Kiraly, and Paula S. Fichtner. 1977.

24. *The Slovenes and Yugoslavism, 1890–1914.* By Carole Rogel. 1977.

25. *German-Hungarian Relations and the Swabian Problem.* By Thomas Spira. 1977.

26. *The Metamorphosis of a Social Class in Hungary During the Reign of Young Franz Joseph.* By Peter I. Hidas. 1977.

27. *Tax Reform in Eighteenth Century Lombardy.* By Daniel M. Klang. 1977.

28. *Tradition versus Revolution: Russia and the Balkans in 1917.* By Robert H. Johnston. 1977.

29. *Winter into Spring: The Czechoslovak Press and the Reform Movement 1963–1968.* By Frank L. Kaplan. 1977.

30. *The Catholic Church and the Soviet Government, 1939–1949.* By Dennis J. Dunn. 1977.

31. *The Hungarian Labor Service System, 1939–1945.* By Randolph L. Braham. 1977.

32. *Consciousness and History: Nationalist Critics of Greek Society 1897–1914.* By Gerasimos Augustinos. 1977.

33. *Emigration in Polish Social and Political Thought, 1870–1914.* By Benjamin P. Murdzek. 1977.

34. *Serbian Poetry and Milutin Bojic.* By Mihailo Dordevic. 1977.

35. *The Baranya Dispute: Diplomacy in the Vortex of Ideologies, 1918–1921.* By Leslie C. Tihany. 1978.

36. *The United States in Prague, 1945–1948.* By Walter Ullmann. 1978.

37. *Rush to the Alps: The Evolution of Vacationing in Switzerland.* By Paul P. Bernard. 1978.

38. *Transportation in Eastern Europe: Empirical Findings.* By Bogdan Mieczkowski. 1978.

39. *The Polish Underground State: A Guide to the Underground, 1939–1945.* By Stefan Korbonski. 1978.

40. *The Hungarian Revolution of 1956 in Retrospect.* Edited by Bela K. Kiraly and Paul Jonas. 1978.

41. *Boleslaw Limanowski (1935–1935): A Study in Socialism and Nationalism.* By Kazimiera Janina Cottam. 1978.

42. *The Lingering Shadow of Nazism: The Austrian Independent Party Movement Since 1945.* By Max E. Riedlsperger. 1978.

43. *The Catholic Church, Dissent and Nationality in Soviet Lithuania.* By V. Stanley Vardys. 1978.

44. *The Development of Parliamentary Government in Serbia.* By Alex N. Dragnich. 1978.

45. *Divide and Conquer: German Efforts to Conclude a Separate Peace, 1914–1918.* By L. L. Farrar, Jr. 1978.

46. *The Prague Slav Congress of 1848.* By Lawrence D. Orton. 1978.

47. *The Nobility and the Making of the Hussite Revolution.* By John M. Klassen. 1978.

48. *The Cultural Limits of Revolutionary Politics: Change and Continuity in Socialist Czechoslovakia.* By David W. Paul. 1979.

49. *On the Border of War and Peace: Polish Intelligence and Diplomacy in 1937–1939 and the Origins of the Ultra Secret.* By Richard A. Woytak. 1979.

50. *Bear and Foxes: The International Relations of the East European States 1965–1969.* By Ronald Haly Linden. 1979.

51. *Czechoslovakia: The Heritage of Ages Past.* Edited by Ivan Volgyes and Hans Brisch. 1979.

52. *Prime Minister Gyula Andrassy's Influence on Habsburg Foreign Policy.* By Janos Decsy. 1979.

53. *Citizens for the Fatherland: Education, Educators, and Pedagogical Ideals in Eighteenth Century Russia.* By J. L. Black. 1979.

54. *A History of the "Proletariat": The Emergence of Marxism in the Kingdom of Poland, 1870–1887.* By Norman M. Naimark. 1979.

55. *The Slovak Autonomy Movement, 1935–1939: A Study in Unrelenting Nationalism.* By Dorothea H. El Mallakh. 1979.

56. *Diplomat in Exile: Francis Pulszky's Political Activities in England, 1849–1860.* By Thomas Kabdebo. 1979.

57. *The German Struggle Against the Yugoslav Guerrillas in World War II: German Counter-Insurgency in Yugoslavia, 1941–1943.* By Paul N. Hehn. 1979.

58. *The Emergence of the Romanian National State.* By Gerald J. Bobango. 1979.

59. *Stewards of the Land: The American Farm School and Modern Greece.* By Brenda L. Marder. 1979.

60. *Roman Dmowski: Party, Tactics, Ideology, 1895–1907.* By Alvin M. Fountain, II. 1980.

61. *International and Domestic Politics in Greece During the Crimean War.* By Jon V. Kofas. 1980.

62. *Fires on the Mountain: The Macedonian Revolutionary Movement and the Kidnapping of Ellen Stone.* By Laura Beth Sherman. 1980.

63. *The Modernization of Agriculture: Rural Transformation in Hungary, 1848–1975.* Edited by Joseph Held. 1980.

64. *Britain and the War for Yugoslavia, 1940–1943.* By Mark C. Wheeler. 1980.

65. *The Turn to the Right: The Ideological Origins and Development of Ukrainian Nationalism, 1919–1929.* By Alexander J. Motyl. 1980.

66. *The Maple Leaf and the White Eagle: Canadian-Polish Relations, 1918–1978.* By Aloysius Balawyder. 1980.

67. *Antecedents of Revolution: Alexander I and the Polish Congress Kingdom, 1815–1825.* By Frank W. Thackeray. 1980.

68. *Blood Libel at Tiszaeszlar.* By Andrew Handler. 1980.

69. *Democratic Centralism in Romania: A Study of Local Communist Politics.* By Daniel N. Nelson. 1980.

70. *The Challenge of Communist Education: A Look at the German Democratic Republic.* By Margrete Siebert Klein. 1980.

71. *The Fortifications and Defense of Constantinople.* By Byron C. P. Tsangadas. 1980.

72. *Balkan Cultural Studies.* By Stavro Skendi. 1980.

73. *Studies in Ethnicity: The East European Experience in America.* Edited by Charles A. Ward, Philip Shashko, and Donald E. Pienkos. 1980.

74. *The Logic of "Normalization:" The Soviet Intervention in Czechoslovakia and the Czechoslovak Response.* By Fred Eidlin. 1980.

75. *Red Cross, Black Eagle: A Biography of Albania's American Schol.* By Joan Fultz Kontos. 1981.

76. *Nationalism in Contemporary Europe.* By Franjo Tudjman. 1981.

77. *Great Power Rivalry at the Turkish Straits: The Montreux Conference and Convention of 1936.* By Anthony R. DeLuca. 1981.

78. *Islam Under the Double Eagle: The Muslims of Bosnia and Hercegovina, 1878–1914.* By Robert J. Donia. 1981.

79. *Five Eleventh Century Hungarian Kings: Their Policies and Their Relations with Rome.* By Z. J. Kosztolnyik. 1981.

80. *Prelude to Appeasement: East European Central Diplomacy in the Early 1930's.* By Lisanne Radice. 1981.

81. *The Soviet Regime in Czechoslovakia.* By Zdenek Krystufek. 1981.

82. *School Strikes in Prussian Poland, 1901–1907: The Struggle Over Bilingual Education.* By John J. Kulczychi. 1981.

83. *Romantic Nationalism and Liberalism: Joachim Lelewel and the Polish National Idea.* By Joan S. Skurnowicz. 1981.

84. *The "Thaw" In Bulgarian Literature.* By Atanas Slavov. 1981.

85. *The Political Thought of Thomas G. Masaryk.* By Roman Szporluk. 1981.

86. *Prussian Poland in the German Empire, 1871–1900.* By Richard Blanke. 1981.

87. *The Mazepists: Ukrainian Separatism in the Early Eighteenth Century.* By Orest Subtelny. 1981.

88. *The Battle for the Marchlands: The Russo-Polish Campaign of 1920.* By Adam Zamoyski. 1981.

89. *Milovan Djilas: A Revolutionary as a Writer.* By Dennis Reinhartz. 1981.

90. *The Second Republic: The Disintegration of Post-Munich Czechoslovakia, October 1938-March 1939.* By Theodore Prochazka, Sr. 1981.

91. *Financial Relations of Greece and the Great Powers, 1832–1862.* By Jon V. Kofas. 1981.

92. *Religion and Politics: Bishop Valerian Trifa and His Times.* By Gerald J. Bobango. 1981.

93. *The Politics of Ethnicity in Eastern Europe.* Edited by George Klein and Milan J. Reban. 1981.

94. *Czech Writers and Politics.* By Alfred French. 1981.

95. *Nation and Ideology: Essays in Honor of Wayne S. Vucinich.* Edited by Ivo Banac, John G. Ackerman, and Roman Szporluk. 1981.

96. *For God and Peter the Great: The Works of Thomas Consett, 1723–1729.* Edited by James Cracraft. 1982.

97. *The Geopolitics of Leninism.* By Stanley W. Page. 1982

98. *Karel Havlicek (1821–1856): A National Liberation Leader of the Czech Renascence.* By Barbara K. Reinfeld. 1982.

99. *Were-Wolf and Vampire in Romania.* By Harry A. Senn. 1982.

100. *Ferdinand I of Austria: The Politics of Dynasticism in the Age of Reformation.* By Paula Sutter Fichtner. 1982

101. *France in Greece During World War I: A Study in the Politics of Power.* By Alexander S. Mitrakos. 1982.

102. *Authoritarian Politics in a Transitional State: Istvan Bethlen and the Unified Party in Hungary, 1919–1926.* By William M. Batkay. 1982.

103. *Romania Between East and West: Historical Essays in Memory of Constantin C. Giurescu.* Edited by Stephen Fischer-Galati, Radu R. Florescu and George R. Ursul. 1982.

104. *War and Society in East Central Europe: From Hunyadi to Rakoczi—War and Society in Late Medieval and Early Modern Hungary.* Edited by János Bak and Béla K. Király. 1982.

105. *Total War and Peace Making: A Case Study on Trianon.* Edited by Béla K. Király, Peter Pastor, and Ivan Sanders. 1982

106. *Army, Aristocracy, and Monarchy: Essays on War, Society, and Government in Austria, 1618–1780.* Edited by Wayne S. Vucinich. 1982.

107. *The First Serbian Uprising, 1804–1813.* Edited by Wayne S. Vucinich. 1982.

108. *Propaganda and Nationalism in Wartime Russia: The Jewish Anti-Fascist Committee in the USSR, 1941–1948.* By Shimon Redich. 1982.

109. *One Step Back, Two Steps Forward: On the Language Policy of the Communist Party of Soviet Union in the National Republics.* By Michael Bruchis. 1982.

110. *Bessarabia and Bukovina: The Soviet-Romanian Territorial Dispute.* by Nicholas Dima. 1982

111. *Greek-Soviet Relations, 1917–1941.* By Andrew L. Zapantis. 1982.

112. *National Minorities in Romania: Change in Transylvania.* By Elemer Illyes. 1982.

113. *Dunarea Noastra: Romania, the Great Powers, and the Danube Question, 1914–1921.* by Richard C. Frucht. 1982.

114. *Continuity and Change in Austrian Socialism: The Eternal Quest for the Third Way.* By Melanie A. Sully. 1982

115. *Catherine II's Greek Prelate: Eugenios Voulgaris in Russia, 1771–1806.* By Stephen K. Batalden. 1982.

116. *The Union of Lublin: Polish Federalism in the Golden Age.* By Harry E. Dembkowski. 1982.

117. *Heritage and Continuity in Eastern Europe: The Transylvanian Legacy in the History of the Romanians.* By Cornelia Bodea and Virgil Candea. 1982.

118. *Contemporary Czech Cinematography: Jiri Menzel and the History of The "Closely Watched Trains".* By Josef Skvorecky. 1982.

119. *East Central Europe in World War I: From Foreign Domination to National Freedom.* By Wiktor Sukiennicki. 1982.

120. *City, Town, and Countryside in the Early Byzantine Era.* Edited by Robert L. Hohlfelder. 1982.

121. *The Byzantine State Finances in the Eighth and Ninth Centuries.* By Warren T. Treadgold. 1982.

122. *East Central European Society and War in Pre-Revolutionary Eighteenth Century.* Edited by Gunther E. Rothenberg, Bela K. Kiraly and Peter F. Sugar. 1982.

123. *Czechoslovak Policy and the Hungarian Minority, 1945–1948.* By Kalman Janics. 1982.

124. *At the Brink of War and Peace: The Tito-Stalin Split in a Historic Perspective.* Edited by Wayne S. Vucinich. 1982.

125. *The Road to Bellapais: The Turkish Cypriot Exodus to Northern Cyprus.* By Pierre Oberling. 1982.

126. *Essays on World War I: Origins and Prisoners of War.* Edited by Peter Pastor and Samuel R. Williamson, Jr. 1983.

127. *Panteleimon Kulish: A Sketch of His Life and Times.* By George S. N. Luckyj. 1983.

128. *Economic Development in the Habsburg Monarchy in the Nineteenth Century: Essays.* Edited by John Komlos. 1983.

129. *Warsaw Between the World Wars: Profile of the Capital City in a Developing Land, 1918–1939.* By Edward D. Wynot, Jr. 1983.

130. *The Lust for Power: Nationalism, Slovakia, and The Communists, 1918–1948.* By Yeshayahu Jelinek. 1983.

131. *The Tsar's Loyal Germans: The Riga German Community: Social Change and the Nationality Question, 1855–1905.* By Anders Henriksson. 1983.

132. *Society in Change: Studies in Honor of Bela K. Kiraly.* Edited by Steven Bela Vardy. 1983.

133. *Authoritariansim in Greece: The Metaxas Regime.* By Jon V. Kofas. 1983.

134. *New Hungarian Peasants: An East Central European Experience with Collectivization.* Edited by Marida Hollos and Bela C. Maday. 1983.

135. *War, Revolution, and Society in Romania: The Road to Independence.* Edited by Ilie Ceausescu. 1983.

136. *The Beginning of Cyrillic Printing, Cracow, 1491: From the Orthodox Past in Poland.* By Szczepan K. Zimmer. 1983.

137. *Effects of World War I. The Class War After the Great War: The Rise of Communist Parties in East Central Europe, 1918–1921.* Edited by Ivo Banac. 1983.

138. *Bulgaria 1878–1918. A History.* By Richard J. Crampton. 1983.

139. *T. G. Masaryk Revisited: A Cirtical Assessment.* By Hanus J. Hajek. 1983.

140. *The Cult of Power: Dictators in the Twentieth Century.* Edited by Joseph Held. 1983.

141. *Economy and Foreign Policy: The Struggle of the Great Powers for Economic Hegemony in the Danube Valley, 1919–1939.* By György Ránki. 1983.

142. *Germany, Russia, and the Balkans: Prelude to the Nazi-Soviet Non-Aggression Pact.* By Marilynn Giroux Hitchens. 1983.

143. **Guestworkers in the German Reich: The Poles in Wilhelmian Germany.** By **Richard Charles Murphy.** 1983.

144. *The Latvian Impact on the Bolshevik Revolution.* By Andrew Ezergailis. 1983.

145. *The Rise of Moscow's Power.* By Henryk Paszkiewicz. 1983.

146. *A Question of Empire: Leopold I and the War of the Spanish Succession, 1701–1705.* By Linda and Marsha Frey. 1983.

147. *Effects of World War I. The Uprooted: Hungarian Refugees and Their Impact on Hungarian Domestic Policies, 1918–1921.* By Istvan I. Mocsy. 1983.

148. *Nationalist Integration Through Socialist Planning: An Anthropological Study of a Romanian New Town.* By Steven L. Sampson. 1983.

149. *Decadence of Freedom: Jacques Riviere's Quest of Russian Mentality.* By Jean-Pierre Cap. 1983.

150. *East Central European Society in the Age of Revolutions, 1775-1856.* Edited by Béla K. Király. 1984.

151. *The Crucial Decade: East Central European Society and National Defense, 1859-1870.* Edited by Béla K. Király. 1984.

152. *The First War between Socialist States: The Hungarian Revolution of 1956 and Its Impact.* Edited by Béla K. Király, Barbara Lotze and Nandor Dreisziger. 1984.

153. *Russian Bolshevism and British Labor, 1917-1921.* By Morton H. Cowden. 1984.

154. *Feliks Dzierzynski and the SDKPIL: A Study of the Origins of Polish Communism.* By Robert Blobaum. 1984.

155. *Studies on Kosova.* Edited by Arshi Pipa and Sami Repishti. 1984.

156. *New Horizons in East-West Economic and Business Relations.* Edited by Marvin A. Jackson and James D. Woodson. 1984.

157. *Czech Nationalism in the Nineteenth Century.* By John F. N. Bradley. 1984.

158. *The Theory of the General Strike from the French Revolution to Poland.* By Phil H. Goodstein. 1984.

159. *King Zog and the Struggle for Stability in Albania.* By Bernd J. Fischer. 1984.

160. *Tradition and Avant-Garde: The Arts in Serbian Culture between the Two World Wars.* By Jelena Milojković-Djurić. 1984.

161. *The Megali Idea and the Greek Turkish War of 1897.* By Theodore G. Tatsios. 1984.

162. *The Hungarian Jewish Catastrophe: A Selected and Annotated Bibliography.* By Randolph L. Braham. 1984.

163. *Goli Otok—Island of Death [A Diary in Letters].* By Venko Markovski. 1984.

164. *Initiation and Initiative: An Exploration of the Life and Ideas of Dimitrije Mitrinovic.* By Andrew Rigby. 1984.

165. *Nations, Nationalities, Peoples: A Study of the Nationality Policies of the Communist Party in Soviet Moldavia.* By Michael Bruchis. 1984.

166. *Frederick I, The Man and His Times.* By Linda and Marsha Frey. 1984.

167. *The Effects of World War I: War Communism in Hungary.* By György Peteri. 1984.